INPUT ENHANCEMENT

From Theory and Research
to the Classroom

The McGraw-Hill Second Language Professional Series

GENERAL EDITORS: James F. Lee and Bill VanPatten

Directions in Second Language Learning and Teaching

Primarily for students of second language acquisition and teaching, curriculum developers, and teacher educators, *Directions in Second Language Learning and Teaching* explores how languages are learned and used and how knowledge about language acquisition and use informs language teaching. The books in this strand emphasize principled approaches to language classroom instruction and management as well as to the education of foreign and second language teachers.

Making Communicative Language Teaching Happen, Second Edition
by James F. Lee and Bill VanPatten, ISBN 0-07-365517-1

Translation Teaching: From Research to the Classroom
by Sonia Colina, ISBN 0-07-248709-7

Gender in the Language Classroom
by Monika Chavez, ISBN 0-07-236749-0

Tasks and Communicating in Language Classrooms
by James F. Lee, ISBN 0-07-231054-5

Affect in Foreign Language and Second Language Learning: A Practical Guide to Creating a Low-Anxiety Classroom Atmosphere
Edited by Dolly Jesusita Young, ISBN 0-07-038900-4

Beyond Methods: Components of Second Language Teacher Education
Edited by Kathleen Bardovi-Harlig and Beverly Hartford, ISBN 0-07-006106-8

Communicative Competence: Theory and Classroom Practice, Second Edition
by Sandra J. Savignon, ISBN 0-07-083736-8

Monographs in Second Language Learning and Teaching

The second strand in the series, *Monographs in Second Language Learning and Teaching,* is designed to provide brief and highly readable texts for beginners and nonspecialists that can be used as supplements to any of the books in the *Directions* strand or with other main texts. An additional goal of the *Monographs* strand is to provide an array of short texts that instructors may combine in various ways to fashion courses that suit their individual needs.

Input Enhancement: From Theory and Research to the Classroom
by Wynne Wong, ISBN 0-07-288725-7

Structured Input: Grammar Instruction for the Acquisition-Oriented Classroom
by Andrew P. Farley, ISBN 0-07-288724-9

Teaching Writing in Second and Foreign Language Classrooms
by Jessica Williams, ISBN 0-07-293479-4

From Input to Output: A Teacher's Guide to Second Language Acquisition
by Bill VanPatten, ISBN 0-07-282561-8

Breaking Tradition: An Exploration of the Historical Relationship between Theory and Practice in Second Language Teaching
by Diane Musumeci, ISBN 0-07-044394-7

INPUT ENHANCEMENT
From Theory and Research to the Classroom

Wynne Wong
The Ohio State University

 **Higher Education**

Boston   Burr Ridge, IL   Dubuque, IA   Madison, WI   New York   San Francisco   St. Louis
Bangkok   Bogotá   Caracas   Kuala Lumpur   Lisbon   London   Madrid   Mexico City
Milan   Montreal   New Delhi   Santiago   Seoul   Singapore   Sydney   Taipei   Toronto

 **Higher Education**

INPUT ENHANCEMENT: FROM THEORY AND RESEARCH TO THE CLASSROOM.

Published by McGraw-Hill, an imprint of The McGraw-Hill Companies, Inc., 1221 Avenue of the Americas, New York, NY 10020. Copyright © 2005. All rights reserved. No part of this publication may be reproduced or distributed in any form or by any means, or stored in a database or retrieval system, without the prior written consent of The McGraw-Hill Companies, Inc., including, but not limited to, in any network or other electronic storage or transmission, or broadcast for distance learning.

This book is printed on acid-free paper.

1 2 3 4 5 6 7 8 9 0 BKM/BKM 0 9 8 7 6 5 4

ISBN 0-07-288725-7

Publisher: *William Glass*
Executive Marketing Manager: *Nick Agnew*
Sponsoring Editor: *William Glass*
Development Editor: *Fionnuala McEvoy*
Project Manager: *Roger Geissler*
Text and Cover Designer: *Violeta Díaz*
Production Supervisor: *Randy Hurst*
Compositor: *Interactive Composition Corporation*
Printer: *Bookmart*

Library of Congress Cataloging-in-Publication Data

Wong, Wynne
    Input enhancement : from theory and research to the classroom / Wynn Wong.
       p. cm. – (The McGraw-Hill second language professional series. Monographs in second langauge learning and teaching)
    Includes bibliographical references and index.
    ISBN 0-07-288725-7 (alk. paper)
    1. Language and languages—Study and teaching. 2. Second language acquisition. I. Title. II. Series

P51.W63 2004
418'.0071 – dc22
                                    2004059732

www.mhhe.com

Noir absolu ou blanc infini
Le silence est la clé
Du langage
Absolute darkness or infinite whiteness
Silence is the key
To language

—Ku Wen Li ◆ Roger Chamberland
(Autumn 2002, *Québec français*, 127)

DEDICATION

This book is dedicated to the cherished memory of Roger Chamberland, an ardent defender of the French language in Québec. His abrupt and tragic departure in June of 2003 sent terrible waves of shock throughout Québec, leaving a void that can never be filled. For those of us whose lives he touched in so many ways, our grief remains heavy.

Roger, I wish you could be here to share this happy moment, the publication of my book, with me. I promise you that la chanson québécoise will resonate loud and clear wherever I go, so loud that it may even reach you through the depths of the thick clouds and the immense sky «comme le son des songes».

Thank you for coloring my life with music.

W.W. (Columbus, October 29, 2003)

l'absence
avec tout le chagrin qui l'accompagne
est la preuve de l'existence
absence
with all the grief that accompanies it
is the proof of existence

—Wynne Wong (Québec, July 7, 2003)

ABOUT THE AUTHOR

Wynne Wong is Assistant Professor of French at The Ohio State University, where she directs the French Basic Language Program. She is Review Editor of Course Materials and Methodology for *The French Review*. Her research area is in second language acquisition. She has published articles and book chapters in the areas of input processing, processing instruction, textual enhancement, language awareness, and the conceptualization of attention in second language acquisition. Her scholarly contributions have appeared in journals such as *Studies in Second Language Acquisition*, *The French Review*, *Foreign Language Annals*, *Acquisition et interaction en langues étrangères (AILE)*, and *Applied Language Learning*. She is the co-recipient of the Stephen A. Freeman Award for Best Published Article on Language Teaching Techniques given by the Northeast Conference on the Teaching of Foreign Languages (2005) for the article "The evidence is IN: Drills are OUT" (*Foreign Language Annals*, 2003). Professor Wong also has an acute interest in Québec cultural studies and has a renowned passion for *la chanson québécoise*.

CONTENTS

ix

FOREWORD

The field of instructed second language acquisition (SLA) has undergone tremendous change since the contemporary era of SLA research began in the late 1960s. With the arrival of work on SLA that yielded results paralleling those from child first language acquisition research, by the late 1970s scholars such as Steven Krashen and Tracy Terrell were calling into question the role of teaching grammar to second language learners. This position stirred considerable debate and the result was a research agenda that has yielded a number of insights into SLA, including the role of input and the effects of formal instruction.

In the present book, Wynne Wong provides the practitioner with the most up-to-date position on formal instruction for language learners. Taking as her starting point the non-controversial position that input is necessary for language acquisition, she discusses various ways in which instruction can enhance what learners get out of the input. This "input enhancement" (a term originally coined by Michael Sharwood Smith) is clearly a far cry from the *hablo, hablas, habla* repetition and substitution drills as well as fill-in-the-blank sheets that have formed the staple of a good deal of language teaching. Focusing on input enhancement, Wong demonstrates just how far the field of instructed SLA has moved in 30 years. By reviewing the research on input enhancement in clear and accessible terms, Wong easily puts the *why* into the hands of practitioners. Her judicious selection of examples to illustrate the various input enhancement techniques provide the *what*, making a splendid volume that unites theory, research and practice in a reader friendly format. An up–and–coming scholar in the field of instructed SLA, Wong has provided the profession with a welcome book. We are very pleased to add it to the McGraw-Hill Second Language Professional Series.

James F. Lee
Bill VanPatten

PREFACE

When people learn that I am a second language acquisition (SLA) researcher and foreign language instructor, the first question they ask is, "So what is the best way to learn a new language?" Upon speaking with them, I often find out that what they really mean by that question is "What is the best way to learn grammar?" And by "grammar learning," they often mean having explicit knowledge about the rules of the new language.

It is not uncommon for people to associate language learning with grammar learning. It is even less uncommon for people to associate grammar instruction with explaining the rules of grammar. If you are reading this book, you were most likely once (and perhaps you still are) a second language (L2) learner yourself and your language learning experience probably involved a lot of explanations about pedagogical grammar rules.

Rule explanation is certainly a form of grammar instruction but as you will see in this book, it is not the only one. Over the years, research in SLA has given us a lot of insight into how people acquire new languages and this research in turn has guided the profession in articulating new approaches and techniques to enhance L2 instruction. One pivotal revelation from SLA research is the following: Learners cannot acquire an L2 without having access to abundant amounts of *input*. What is input? Input is L2 language data that learners are exposed to in a communicative context or setting. We have all probably heard at one time or another that the best way to learn a new language is to live in the country where that language is spoken. Why is that? The answer lies in the opportunities that such a learning context provides for us to receive input. When we live in the target language country, we are constantly exposed to input in that country's language. Every time we listen to people on the street, or mingle with friends or watch TV, we are receiving input to set the processes of SLA in motion.

No matter what theoretical framework or context SLA researchers work from, there is no dispute that acquisition cannot happen without exposure to ample amounts of input. All SLA scholars are in agreement today that input is an essential ingredient of successful SLA. This fundamental "discovery" significantly altered the way in which the profession conceptualized how languages are acquired. This in turn has led to new conceptualizations about what effective grammar instruction may look like.

WHAT IS THIS BOOK ABOUT? WHAT IS ITS PURPOSE?

This book is about grammar instruction that works with what learners need for successful SLA: Input. The purpose of this book is to introduce readers to instructional techniques that help L2 learners pay attention to grammatical form while also providing them with the comprehensible input they need for acquisition at the same time. These techniques are called *input enhancement* techniques. Input enhancement was a term first coined by Michael Sharwood Smith to refer to instructional interventions that make target grammatical forms more salient so that learners will be more likely to pay attention to them. I am using this term in my book to refer to instructional techniques that rely on input as their foundation for instruction. These techniques are input flood, textual enhancement, structured input activities and grammar consciousness-raising (GCR) tasks. After reading this book, you should:

- understand the important role that input plays in second language acquisition;
- have a working knowledge of the basic theoretical underpinnings and research findings that motivate the use of input enhancement techniques;
- be familiar with the input enhancement techniques presented;
- know how to implement these different input enhancement techniques in your own classrooms.

WHO IS THIS BOOK FOR?

This book assumes no prior knowledge of second language acquisition. The tone and style taken in the book are purposefully informal and are meant to be reader friendly. It is intended for those who are beginning or have already begun a teaching career. It can be read by undergraduates pursuing certification, graduate students in methods courses and in-service instructors who wish to explore and/or expand their knowledge base of different input enhancement techniques as well as to understand the theoretical and research implications of such techniques.

This book can be read with profit in a number of contexts:

- It can stand alone as the text to a course that focuses on different types of classroom interventions in instructed SLA
- It can stand alone as the text to a course that explores possible ways that L2 learners' attention could be drawn to form in acquisition-rich L2 learning environments such as content-based instruction and other communicative rich environments

- It can serve as an adjunct to a number of "methods" books used in introductory language teaching courses (e.g., Lee & VanPatten, 2003; Omaggio-Hadley, 2001)
- It can be used in conjunction with other introductory books on SLA (e.g., Spada & Lightbown, 1999; VanPatten, 2003)

ORGANIZATION AND FEATURES

This book is organized into eight chapters. Chapter 1 provides a historical overview of grammar instruction in order to situate the context for input enhancement. Chapter 2 explains what SLA research is and defines what acquisition means in terms of ten generalizations about the nature of acquisition. The second part of this chapter discusses the relationship between SLA research and real-world teaching. A discussion on how instructors should approach the application of research findings to the classroom is included. Chapter 3 focuses on the role of input in SLA and how learners get linguistic data from input in order to provide a theoretically sound rationale for the use of input enhancement in the classroom. Chapters 4–7 are devoted to detailed discussions of actual input enhancement techniques: input flood (Chapter 4), textual enhancement (Chapter 5), structured input activities (Chapter 6), and grammar consciousness-raising (GCR) tasks (Chapter 7). Each chapter begins with a definition of the technique and how the technique is carried out. This is followed by a concise review of selected relevant research in a non-technical manner to show what the technique could be expected to do. A discussion on the advantages and disadvantages of each technique is provided followed by suggestions on how to implement the technique in actual language classrooms. Each chapter concludes with sample materials from a variety of languages (e.g., English, French, German, Italian, Romanian, Russian, Spanish) to give instructors good models for material development. Finally, Chapter 8 brings all the techniques together by addressing issues such as (1) how to choose the appropriate technique for different classroom needs, (2) how these techniques may be integrated into different types of classrooms, (3) how to assess whether input enhancement techniques have been successful, and (4) the role of output in SLA and other types of pedagogical interventions.

Within each chapter, you will also find boxes entitled *Pause to Consider . . .* dispersed throughout the text. These boxes are intended to help readers reflect on some of the topics that are discussed in the text. When you come across these boxes, you are invited to stop and ponder a particular issue. If you are using this book in a class, these boxes could be used as springboards for discussion.

At the end of each chapter, you will find a section called *Enhance Your Knowledge*. This section contains full references to primary reading sources that are related to the topic at hand. You will also find a complete reference section at the end of the book as well as a glossary of key terms and concepts that appear in boldface type within chapters.

ACKNOWLEDGMENTS

I want to first thank my students for constantly reminding me why I chose this profession and why I love what I do so much. Thank you for giving me the privilege of sharing what I love with you. You are my inspiration for this book.

I am grateful to James F. Lee and Bill VanPatten, the general editors, for giving my ideas a home in their series. I hope we will have many more opportunities to work together.

Thanks are also due to William R. Glass, my publisher, Lindsay Eufusia and Fionnuala McEvoy, the editors, and all the people at McGraw-Hill who made this book possible, particularly the Editorial, Design and Production team: Roger Geissler, Violeta Diaz, Randy Hurst and Louis Swaim.

I want to thank the outside reviewers who examined the proposal and sample chapter of this book. They are Rebecca Peterson, Leila Ranta, and Kate Wolfe-Quintero. Their questions and comments helped me refine my ideas and ultimately pushed me to produce a better final product.

Special thanks go to Bill VanPatten. Thank you for making everything we do so much fun and for adding that *je ne sais quoi* to our profession.

Special thanks also go to Daphnée Simard for taking time out of her busy schedule to read different parts of my manuscript for me. I'm so glad we met at that *méchoui* in Québec what now seems like so many years ago. We will always make time to work together.

Many, many thanks to the individuals who helped me write and translate some of the sample materials in this book. They are Joe Barcroft, Nicoleta Bazgan, Alessia Colarossi, Justin Ehrenberg, Adriana Golumbeanu, Olga Levin, and Dorothée Mertz. I am VERY grateful to all of you! Thanks also go to Alessandro Benati, An Cheng, Drew Farley, Renée Jourdenais, Michael Leeser, Mark Overstreet, Susanne Rott, and Daphnée Simard for graciously allowing me to use their materials.

Finally, I would like to thank the following people whose love and emotional support carried me through the completion of this book: Joe Barcroft, Renée Gosson, Claude Grégoire, Deirdre Heistad, Anne Lair, Daphnée Simard, Bill VanPatten and Monsieur Émile. You all helped me more than you can ever know. I don't want to miss any opportunities to tell you how much I love and appreciate you. *Un peu plus haut, un peu plus loin . . . Encore un pas, un petit pas, encore un saut et je suis là—C'est beau.*

Wynne Wong
Columbus, October 28, 2003

From Grammar-Translation to Input Enhancement: A Historical Overview of Grammar Instruction

One of the questions that instructors in training usually want to ask during their training workshop or methodology course is, "How should we teach grammar?" This question should not come as a surprise given that adult learners and even instructors tend to view grammar as the central component of any given language. Furthermore, if we examined the plethora of second language (L2)[1] instruction methods that have surfaced over the course of history, we would see that discussions of the role of grammar have always been pertinent to the articulation of each teaching methodology. In this chapter, we explore some of the different positions that grammar has held in various teaching approaches and methodologies. Because the volume of these different methods is overwhelming, we will only concentrate on a select few that have made a significant impact on the history of language teaching.[2]

The Sixteenth to Nineteenth Centuries: The Grammar-Translation Method

When talking about the history of language teaching, many authors take the sixteenth century as the starting point with a method that would become known as the **Grammar-Translation Method.** Prior to the sixteenth century, Latin was the most widely studied language. Like English is for us today, Latin at that time was the primary language of commerce, religion and education. However, political changes in Europe during the sixteenth century changed the status of Latin in the Western world. As languages such as French, Italian, and English gained in importance, Latin was no longer regarded as the language of written or oral communication. After the sixteenth century, Latin was reduced to a mere subject matter for academic study. People studied Latin for the sole purpose of reading classical literature (e.g., Virgil, Ovid, and Cicero) and to develop intellectual ability. In order to read and appreciate the great literary works written in Latin, it was believed that students needed to have a thorough knowledge of grammatical rules (in both their first and second languages) and to be able to translate texts from their L2 to their first language (L1) and

2

CHAPTER 1
*From Grammar-
Translation to Input
Enhancement:
A Historical
Overview of
Grammar Instruction*

vice versa. Thus, L2 study at this time mainly consisted of rote learning of grammatical rules and memorization of declensions and verb conjugations. Virtually no attention was given to aural comprehension or speaking proficiency. Practice activities primarily consisted of translation exercises. If students could translate something accurately, then it was assumed that they learned the grammar well.

Modern languages appeared in European school curriculums in the late nineteenth and early twentieth centuries. Because the Grammar-Translation Method was the most well-known method at the time, this method was also used to teach these modern languages. While the Grammar-Translation Method began to decline around the nineteenth century, we can still see traces of it today in language courses where reading knowledge of an L2 is critical (e.g., courses for graduate students who need to pass a reading proficiency exam in an L2).

The Nineteenth Century: The Direct Method

Around the mid-nineteenth century, a demand for oral proficiency in foreign languages increased as communication became more and more important among Europeans. This demand for oral proficiency motivated educators to question and eventually reject the Grammar-Translation Method as this method did not develop any kind of functional ability in language learners. Educators began to look for alternative methods of language teaching drawing on knowledge sources from linguistics and child language acquisition. This became known as the reform movement in the mid-to-late nineteenth century (Richards & Rodgers, 2001). Because communication was now the primary goal for language study (as opposed to the reading of classical works), much emphasis would be placed on oral proficiency and the here-and-now.

The most widely cited method during this period of reform was a method called the **Direct Method.** Drawing on principles from child L1 acquisition, advocates of this method believed that people learned languages by listening to it in large quantities and by making direct associations of words and phrases with the meaning they represent (Larsen-Freeman, 1986). Under this method, classroom instruction was to be conducted exclusively in the L2. Because of the emphasis on oral communication and the here-and-now, only common everyday vocabulary and sentences were taught. Pictures, gestures and objects were generally used to present concrete vocabulary while more abstract vocabulary was presented via paraphrasing. Unlike the Grammar-Translation Method, grammar was not explicitly taught. Students were instead encouraged to arrive at their own generalizations about grammar from examples and language practice activities. In other words, learners were expected to induce the rules of grammar on their own. The rationale behind this approach to grammar instruction was based on observations from child L1 acquisition. Because it was believed that children learned grammar through interpreting contextual and situational cues (rather than through explicit explanations), advocates of the Direct Method held the position that grammar was best taught inductively.

3

CHAPTER 1
From Grammar-
Translation to Input
Enhancement:
A Historical
Overview of
Grammar Instruction

> *Pause to consider . . .*
>
> the nature of L1 and L2 learning. The Direct Method was in part based on the assumption that L1 and L2 learning are similar. What do you think about this assumption? In what ways are L1 and L2 learning similar? In what ways are they different?

The Direct Method declined around the 1920s but we can still see this method actively used in some commercial schools today where speaking proficiency in an L2 is necessary for career or travel purposes. In the United States, this method is known as the Berlitz Method.

Regardless of whether one subscribes to the principles of the Direct Method or not, this method had a significant impact on the history of L2 instruction because it represented the first attempt to teach language in a principled manner. Richards and Rodgers (2001) associate the Direct Method with the birth of the concept of a teaching methodology. When the Direct method made its entrance in foreign language teaching circles, educators were stimulated to question and debate the nature of language learning. This in turn led to the development of many different methods and approaches to language instruction throughout the twentieth century, especially from the 1950s to the 1980s. Not all of the methods that came out of this period would have a durable impact on the language teaching profession. One method that did have a lasting influence was a method called the Audiolingual Method.

The 1950s–: The Audiolingual Method

The **Audiolingual Method** (ALM) was born out of two academic disciplines that were influential during the 1950s: behaviorist psychology and structural linguistics. According to behaviorist psychology, all learning, that is to say, both verbal and non-verbal, was the result of habit formation. Habits were believed to be formed through the process of repetition, imitation, and reinforcement. Under ALM, the goal of language instruction was to instill in learners the same habits (i.e., linguistic abilities) that native speakers have via stimulus-response techniques. This was carried out by having learners memorize dialogues and practice pattern drills. Students were rarely given the opportunity to create language because they could make errors and these errors might lead to forming incorrect language habits that may be difficult to eradicate. Influenced by the tenet of structural linguistics that language is primarily an oral phenomena, aural-oral training was emphasized over the written modality. Grammar was considered an important component of ALM. Based on the belief that learning was a result of habit formation, proponents of this method advocated teaching grammar through analogy rather than analysis. In other words, learners should not have to think about rules of grammar. Grammar is best taught by having students produce grammatically correct

4

CHAPTER 1
From Grammar-
Translation to Input
Enhancement:
A Historical
Overview of
Grammar Instruction

sentences via pattern drills. The idea was that if learners received sufficient practice in producing correct language structures, they would eventually internalize these grammatical forms. Thus, grammar was not taught explicitly under ALM. Learners were expected to get grammatical knowledge through sufficient amounts of pattern practice.

The Late 1960s–: Cognitive-Code Method

By the late 1960s and early 1970s, the behaviorist view of language learning was called into question. Influenced by Chomsky's linguistic theory and cognitive psychologists such as Lenneberg (1964) and Ausubel (1968), language was now viewed as a rule-governed entity and meaningful language learning was advocated over rote learning. During this period, there was a shift from an emphasis on analogy to an emphasis on analysis in language learning. Rather than mimic language structures, the belief was that learners needed to understand and analyze the rules of language in order to build linguistic competence. This new view of language learning was best exemplified in a method known as the **Cognitive-Code Method.**

Under the Cognitive-Code Method, learning was believed not to be a result of habit formation but to be an analytical process that moved from previously acquired knowledge to unknown knowledge (See Chastain, 1976, for a description of the major tenets of this method). Thus, language learning needed to be meaningful so that learners could understand what they were learning and saying. Instructional materials needed to be organized around what students already knew so they could relate new information to their existing knowledge. As for grammar instruction, proponents of this method believed that the learning of grammar required mental processing and was too complex to be learned by association alone. Learners should thus be encouraged to understand the grammatical system of their L2 rather than merely memorize and repeat surface strings in a rote manner. Creative use of language was encouraged but only after learners were familiar with the rules of the L2. Thus, under the Cognitive-Code Method, the language teaching profession observed a renewed interest in explicit grammar instruction.

The 1980s–: Communicative Language Teaching

The 1980s marked the advent of an approach to L2 instruction known as **communicative language teaching** (CLT),[3] an approach that is widely used today in North America and Europe among other places. We say that CLT is an approach and not a method because it is defined in terms of a teaching philosophy rather than a set of prescribed procedures. As an approach, CLT aims to make communicative competence the goal of L2 instruction and to help instructors articulate procedures for teaching that take into consideration the interdependence of language and communication (Richards & Rodgers, 2001). Many factors motivated the development of CLT: (a) the rising need to learn foreign languages for communicative purposes as a result of the increasing interdependence of European countries; (b) the influence of humanist ideas of learning in the late seventies and early eighties; and (c) the realization that pattern practice (as was typical with ALM) and explicit knowledge of grammar rules (as advocated by cognitive approaches) did not produce learners who could use their L2s in a communicative fashion. Drawing on readings from Canale and Swain (1980), Rivers (1987), Savignon (1998), and others, VanPatten (2002) describes CLT in terms of the following tenets:

5

CHAPTER *1*
*From Grammar-
Translation to Input
Enhancement:
A Historical
Overview of
Grammar Instruction*

1. *Meaning should always be in focus.* In general CLT, the expression, interpretation, and negotiation of meaning within the classroom context is the primary focus.
2. *Learners should be at the center of the curriculum.* First, the needs and interests of L2 learners should inform the curriculum about relevant topics and themes whenever possible. Second, knowledge about how learners acquire languages (i.e., research in SLA) should inform methodology and materials development.
3. *Communication is not only oral but written and gestural as well.* Thus, CLT should use a broad set of materials (audio, visual, video) and should encourage the development of skills appropriate to learner interests and needs.
4. *Samples of authentic language used among native speakers should be available from the beginning of instruction.* This is not limited to conversations. It is intended to include written and oral texts from a variety of sources (e.g., television, magazines, newspapers, etc.).
5. *Communicative events in class should be purposeful.* This means that tasks should foster the learning of new information about members of the class and the world around them or at the very least serve as goals for instruction.

(adapted from VanPatten, 2002)

Pause to consider . . .

the tenets of CLT. What teaching methods or instructional activities that you know of are a reflection of the tenets of CLT?

What about the role of grammar in CLT? You may have noticed that the tenets of CLT described above do not mention how grammar should be taught. This should not be taken to mean that grammatical competence is not considered to be important[4]. The reason why we do not see an explicit statement about grammar instruction in the tenets of CLT is because CLT is not a teaching method. As we described earlier, CLT is an approach that may encompass many different methods. **Content-based instruction,** for example, where the L2 is used as the medium of communication (as opposed to the object of study) for subject matter learning, is one method stemming from CLT.

6

CHAPTER *1*
From Grammar-
Translation to Input
Enhancement:
A Historical
Overview of
Grammar Instruction

> ## *Pause to consider . . .*
>
> content-based instruction. How is content-based instruction a communicative approach?

In short, CLT is about adhering to a particular set of beliefs about the nature of language learning, that is to say, that language is intricately tied to the act of communication. Many teaching techniques could be used to realize the tenets of CLT described above including grammar instruction in some form. However, in what is sometimes known as the "strong" form of CLT, grammar instruction tended to be downplayed and in some cases, completely eradicated from the classroom. Hinkel and Fotos (2002) describe communicative approaches to language instruction as instruction that does not include "formal grammar instruction" or "the correction of learner errors" (pp. 4–5). Learners are instead presented with large quantities of "meaning-focused input containing target forms and vocabulary" (p. 4). Therefore, under the strong view of CLT, grammar instruction was virtually absent from L2 classrooms (even though this was not prescribed in the tenets of CLT).

This apprehension of including grammar in CLT classrooms could in part be a response to the tendency toward grammar overkill used in earlier methods that did not help learners develop any kind of communicative ability in the L2. Another reason may also be attributed to the theoretical position articulated by Krashen in the seventies and eighties that languages are acquired via exposure to comprehensible input alone. Krashen was not directly associated with CLT but many of his ideas about the nature of language acquisition and L2 instruction were compatible with the tenets of CLT.

Krashen's Hypotheses

Krashen (1982) makes a distinction between two independent processes of developing competence in an L2: acquisition (also called acquired competence) and learning (or learned competence). He defines **acquisition** as a subconscious process of language development very much like the process by which children acquire their L1. **Learning** refers to a conscious knowledge of the rules of grammar that is a product of instruction. According to Krashen, learning can never become acquisition and it is acquisition that is responsible for the development of learners' internal linguistic system. Learning is only useful as a way of helping learners edit their speech when they have time to think about the grammar rules that they need to apply. According to Krashen, acquisition occurs when learners are exposed to comprehensible input. If learners have access to an optimal amount of appropriate comprehensible input, then acquisition should just happen naturally. We will discuss the concept of input and the role that it plays in SLA in detail in Chapter 3. For now, you should understand that input refers to samples of language in the L2 that contains some kind of message that the learner is supposed to comprehend. For Krashen, "appropriate" input is input that contains structures (lexis, morphology, syntax, etc.) just one step beyond the learners' current stage of linguistic development. He refers to this as $i + 1$ (input plus structures at one stage beyond). According to Krashen (1983), learners can *understand* these unknown structures by relying on their world knowledge, their previously acquired linguistic knowledge and extra-linguistic contexts such as pictures and other visuals. When learners receive enough input and understand it, acquisition is "unavoidable" and "cannot be prevented" (Krashen, 1985, p. 4). Formal grammar instruction, in Krashen's view, is unnecessary for acquisition.

Pause to consider . . .

Krashen's position. Do you know of anyone (from history, TV or people you know) who learned an L2 via input alone, that is to say, without any formal instruction?

Krashen made a significant contribution to the field of SLA by underscoring the important role of input in language acquisition (a point we will discuss in greater detail in Chapter 3). However, his views have also been criticized as being untestable and unrealistic for application in actual classrooms. For example, just how much comprehensible input is optimal for SLA? This is extremely difficult to investigate and Krashen remains vague on this point. Furthermore, the unfortunate reality of most classroom learning contexts is that comprehensible input tends not to be as abundant as we would hope (see Wing, 1987, for a discussion on this point). Another source of skepticism comes from research on French immersion programs in Canada. In these programs, students often learned a variety of academic subjects in the L2 so they were exposed to a highly concentrated amount of input. Unfortunately, this research shows that even after years of exposure to comprehensible input in the L2, learners still could not reach certain levels of accuracy for certain grammatical features (e.g., Harley, 1993; Harley & Swain, 1984; Lightbown & Spada, 1990; Swain, 1985, 1995). These findings motivated the language profession to re-evaluate the role of grammar in L2 classrooms. There was no debate that input was crucial to SLA but researchers began to postulate that input alone may not be sufficient for some if not many learning contexts.

INPUT ENHANCEMENT

Sharwood Smith (1981, 1991) introduced the concept of input enhancement (first known as "consciousness-raising") as a way of reorienting the discussion on the role of grammar in L2 instruction. **Input enhancement,** in Sharwood Smith's definition, refers to a deliberate attempt to make specific features of L2 input more salient in order to draw learners' attention to these features (1991, p. 118). Reacting against the position that grammar instruction had little or no use in the L2 classroom, a position most often associated with Krashen (1981, 1985) and the strong form of CLT, Sharwood Smith sought to redefine the notion of formal grammar instruction. Sharwood Smith points out that one of the reasons why drawing learners' attention to the formal properties of an L2

8

CHAPTER 1
From Grammar-
Translation to Input
Enhancement:
A Historical
Overview of
Grammar Instruction

has been viewed in a negative light is because formal instruction has often been associated with "the pedantic giving and testing of rules and lists of vocabulary items" (1981, p. 160). This view, however, needs to be modified because there are many ways to help learners pay attention to the formal properties of language that need not involve detailed metalinguistic discussion. Sharwood Smith and his colleague Rutherford offer the following as examples of the varied nature of input enhancement:

> There are many ways of drawing attention to form without indulging in metalinguistic discussion. A simple example would be the use of typographical conventions such as underlining or capitalizing a particular grammatical surface feature, where you merely ask the learners to pay attention to anything that is underlined or capitalized. Another example would be the deliberate exposure of the learner to an artificially large number of instances of some target structure in the language on the assumption that the very high frequency of the structure in question will attract the learner's attention to the relevant formal regularities.
>
> —Rutherford & Sharwood Smith, 1985, p. 271

The techniques that Rutherford and Sharwood Smith described above are called "input enhancement" because input is enhanced to make certain features more salient. Sharwood Smith (1981, 1991) further explains that different input enhancement techniques may vary in degrees of explicitness and elaboration. **Explicitness** refers to the sophistication and detail of the attention-drawing device. At the highly explicit end of the continuum, one might find metalinguistically sophisticated rule explanation. At the less explicit end, the device might be in the form of a facial gesture or seeing the target form highlighted. **Elaboration** refers to the depth and amount of time that is involved in implementing the enhancement technique. Taking the facial gesture as an example, if an instructor frowned only once when a mistake was made, that would be an example of a less elaborate signal. By contrast, if the instructor frowned each time the learner made a mistake, then that signal could be characterized as more elaborate.

The point that Sharwood Smith wanted to make in his discussion of input enhancement was that metalinguistic discussion represented only one way of getting learners to pay attention to grammar. Recognizing the need to help learners pay attention to the formal aspects of an L2 does not necessarily mean a return to lengthy grammatical explanations or rote learning.

Pause to consider . . .

the varying degrees of explicitness and elaboration of input enhancement techniques. On what basis should instructors decide whether a "signal" should be more or less elaborate, or more or less explicit? Can you think of some concrete examples?

Sharwood Smith cautions that while input enhancement is presumed to increase the chances that learners will attend to a target form, this does not mean that they actually will. Furthermore, even if learners do pay attention to the enhanced form, there is no guarantee that they will internalize the form (Sharwood Smith, 1991, p. 122). It was for this reason that Sharwood Smith replaced his earlier term "consciousness-raising" with "input enhancement."

Input Enhancement and Focus-On-Form

As Sharwood Smith was articulating his ideas about input enhancement, other researchers such as Long were also taking a second look at the role of grammar instruction. A study by Long (1983) comparing a certain population of naturalistic learners (i.e., learners who did not receive formal instruction in the L2) with classroom learners demonstrated that those who received some kind of formal instruction tended to have an advantage. This prompted Long and others to conclude that formal instruction could enhance foreign language learning, provided of course, that it takes place within communicative contexts.

Concerned that the renewed interest in form-focused instruction might result in a diminished role for meaningful language use in the classroom, Long (1991) made a distinction between two types of pedagogic interventions: focus-on-form and focus-on-forms. In Long's definition, **focus-on-form** refers to techniques that draw learners' attention to form within a meaningful context as the need arises whereas **focus-on-forms** draws learners' attention to isolated language forms either separately from meaning or with no apparent regard for meaning. What Long was advocating of course was *focus-on-form* and not *focus-on-forms*: "Focus on form . . . overtly draws students' attention to linguistic elements as they arise incidentally in lessons whose overriding focus is on meaning or communication" (1991, pp. 45–46).

Focus-on-form is similar to input enhancement in that both refer to external efforts to draw learners' attention to form. However, while focus-on-form techniques require that the technique occur incidentally during communicative events, input enhancement does not. In Long's original use of the term, focus-on-form would exclude pedagogical practices that require a proactive as opposed to a reactive response to attention to form. Input enhancement, as Sharwood Smith uses it, is less restrictive because it can be both proactive and reactive and does not require communicative interaction as a prerequisite. However, as Spada (1997) and Doughty and Williams (1998) point out, scholars today tend to use the term "focus-on-form" in a broader sense and have expanded it to include both proactive and reactive types of interaction. As used today, focus-on-form may refer to any technique that is used to draw learners' attention to form in classrooms within meaning-based approaches and may occur either spontaneously or in predetermined ways. In this expanded definition of focus-on-form, it is quite similar to input enhancement. This book, however, adopts the term input enhancement instead of focus-on-form in an effort to underscore the fundamental role that input must play in any instructional technique.

10

CHAPTER 1
From Grammar-
Translation to Input
Enhancement:
A Historical
Overview of
Grammar Instruction

Pause to consider . . .

focus-on-form and focus-on-forms activities. What activities can you think of that could be classified as focus-on-form? Can you give examples of activities that would go under the category of focus-on-forms as defined by Long?

SUMMARY/CONCLUSION

As this historical overview demonstrates, the role of grammar in L2 instruction has always been important to the articulation of various teaching methods over the centuries and in recent years. As purposes for L2 learning and ideas about the nature of language acquisition evolved over the course of history, so did the face of grammar instruction. In the methods that we sampled, grammar has been presented explicitly and deductively most often in the form of rule explanations (e.g., Grammar-Translation Method, Cognitive-Code Method), as well as more inductively via direct associations (e.g., Direct Method) and pattern drills (ALM). We have witnessed some extreme positions ranging from the idea that grammar should be the object of study (e.g., Grammar-Translation Method) to the proposal that grammar instruction should be completely eliminated from the classroom (e.g., strong form of CLT). Today, after four decades or so of research in SLA, few would argue that drawing learners' attention to grammatical form in some way is at least beneficial for many L2 learning contexts. As Sharwood Smith and others have pointed out, there are many ways to draw learners' attention to form without compromising opportunities for meaningful interaction in the classroom. Furthermore, the years of accumulated research evidence appears to support this practice. Today, the general consensus regarding grammar instruction is that it may be useful provided that it is carried out within communicative and meaningful contexts and as long as it is based on what we know about how languages are acquired. In the next chapter, we will discuss why instructors should turn to SLA theory and research to help them make informed pedagogical choices.

CHAPTER NOTES

1. Some scholars make a distinction between foreign language acquisition, that is, learning a language in an environment where the target language is not the primary language (e.g., learning French in the United States) and second language acquisition, that is, learning a language in an environment where that language is spoken (e.g., learning Spanish in Mexico). Unless otherwise noted, the term second language (L2) is used in this book to refer to any language that is not a learner's first language (L1) regardless of context. Thus, learning French in the U.S. and learning Spanish in Mexico are both considered L2 learning.
2. Some of the methods that are not presented in this chapter include Community Language Learning, The Lexical Approach, Neurolinguistic Programming, The Silent

Way, Situational Language Teaching, Suggestopedia, Total Physical Response, and Whole Language Learning. See Richards and Rodgers (2001) for detailed descriptions of these methods.
3. The profession generally identifies the 1980s with the advent of CLT. However, taking a historical approach, Musumeci (1997) points out that the principles underlying CLT go back as far as the fifteenth century with an educator named Guarino Guarini.
4. Canale (1983), Canale and Swain (1980), and Savignon (1998) define communicative competence as consisting of four underlying competences: (1) grammatical competence, (2) discourse competence, (3) sociolinguistic competence, and (4) strategic competence.

ENHANCE YOUR KNOWLEDGE

Techniques and Approaches to Language Instruction

Larsen-Freeman, D. (1986). *Techniques and principles in language teaching*. Oxford: Oxford University Press.

Richards, J. C., & Rodgers, T. S. (2001). *Approaches and methods in language teaching* (2nd edition). Cambridge: Cambridge University Press.

Historical Perspectives

Germain, C. (1993). *Évolution de l'enseignement des langues: 5000 ans d'histoire*. Paris: CLE international.

Musumeci, D. (1997). *Breaking tradition*. New York: McGraw-Hill.

Communicative Language Teaching

Lee, J. F., & VanPatten, B. (2003). *Making communicative language teaching happen (2nd edition)*. New York: McGraw-Hill.

Savignon. S. (1998). *Communicative competence: Theory and classroom practice* (2nd edition). New York: McGraw-Hill.

Input Enhancement

Sharwood Smith, M. (1981). Consciousness raising and the second language learner. *Applied Linguistics, 2*, 159–168.

Sharwood Smith, M. (1991). Speaking to many minds: On the relevance of different types of language information. *Second Language Research, 7*, 118–132.

Sharwood Smith, M. (1993). Input enhancement in instructed SLA: Theoretical bases. *Studies in Second Language Acquisition, 15*, (2), 165–79.

Second Language Acquisition Theory, Research, and Real-World Teaching

Toute pratique pédagogique peut s'enrichir par l'explication de ses principes.
All pedagogical practice may be enriched by the explanation of its principles.

—Daniel Gaonac'h (1987)

WHAT IS SECOND LANGUAGE ACQUISITION ABOUT?

As an academic discipline, the field of second language acquisition (SLA) is concerned with explaining how people acquire a language other than their first language (L1) both inside and outside the classroom (e.g., immigrants learning French in Québec, a college student learning a third foreign language at a university, a study abroad student learning Italian in Italy, etc.). SLA is thus not language or context specific. SLA is a theory-building field that draws on disciplines such as linguistics, cognitive psychology and psycholinguistics among others. SLA researchers build theories about the processes that underlie how people acquire L2s and rely on empirical evidence to support these theories.

Instructors-in-training who are not familiar with the field of SLA sometimes think that this discipline is concerned with teaching methodology and that the job of SLA specialists is to design effective instructional materials. While it is true that many SLA researchers are interested in the effects of formal language instruction, this is not the primary concern of the field. SLA researchers do not typically deal with day-to-day classroom instruction issues such as "what is the best way to correct compositions" or "what is the best way to teach direct object pronouns." SLA researchers and theorists are concerned with investigating whether instruction has any effect on acquisition in the first place. Can instruction alter the processes that learners use to internalize a new language? Here are some additional questions that SLA researchers attempt to investigate and answer (adapted from Kramsch, 2000,

- How does acquisition of a second language occur, that is to say, how do learners of a native language internalize the linguistic system of another language?
- What does their second language look like? What kinds of errors do they make?
- To what extent are language structures transferred from the L1?
- What factors affect acquisition?
- Does formal instruction have an impact on SLA?
- How does fluency develop?
- What role is played by sociocultural factors such as affect, motivation, and the desire to identify with the native speaker?

Such questions guide SLA researchers as they construct theories and design research experiments to test these theories. As you can see, the role of instruction in SLA is just one of many questions that SLA researchers investigate.

What Is Acquisition?

Because the volume of SLA research is so vast, it will not be possible to go into a thorough discussion about the nature of SLA in this chapter. In the next sections, we will discuss some accepted generalizations about SLA drawn from SLA theory and research that may be considered to be most pertinent for L2 instructors. Lightbown first outlined these generalizations in two research articles (Lightbown, 1985, 2000) to help instructors understand the nature of acquisition, and to help them set realistic expectations for L2 instruction.

Adults and Adolescents Can "Acquire" a Second Language

Lightbown uses the term "acquisition" to refer to the distinction that Krashen (1982) (discussed in Chapter 1) first made between linguistic abilities that learners develop unconsciously in the absence of metalinguistic instruction (acquisition), and knowledge that they have about the L2 that is a result of explicit formal instruction (learning). When Lightbown says that adults and adolescents can "acquire" an L2, she means that there are features of an L2 that learners may acquire *incidentally* without intentional effort or formal instruction (2000, p. 439). VanPatten (2003) adds that much of SLA involves the creation of an **implicit linguistic system** that lies outside of awareness. All native speakers of a language have an implicit linguistic system. We say that this linguistic system is implicit because native speakers are generally unaware of the properties that govern this system. For example, native speakers of English know that it is possible to say *Who do you wanna go with?* but that it is not possible to say *Who do you wanna bring the beer to the picnic?* but they cannot explain why. When we take on the task of acquiring an L2, we are in the process of developing a new implicit linguistic system. Research evidence demonstrates that even in the early stages of SLA, L2 learners possess an implicit linguistic system that functions in a very similar manner as that of native speakers. When asked to judge the correctness of L2 sentences, including sentences that contain structures that have never been taught via instruction or feedback, L2 learners can usually come up with the correct answers even though they cannot explain why an individual sentence is correct or incorrect (see VanPatten & Mandell, 1999). The finding that L2 learners can come to know things about their L2 that have never been taught to them has led researchers and theorists in the field of SLA to posit a primary role for what is called **input,** a point we will discuss in detail later in the next chapter.

Pause to consider . . .

your implicit L2 system. Can you recall examples from your own L2 learning experience where you intuitively knew a sentence or structure was incorrect but you could not explain why?

The Learner Creates a Systematic Interlanguage

The term **interlanguage** was coined by Selinker (1972) to refer to the systematic knowledge that learners have of their L2 at any given point in time during their L2 development. In other words, it is what the learners' implicit linguistic system looks like at any given stage of development. When we say that this interlanguage is 'systematic,' we mean that this knowledge source cannot be explained by the type of instruction or input that learners are exposed to. Lightbown (1991, 2000) points out that even when learners are explicitly taught and given a lot of practice with specific L2 structures, they create their own systematic interlanguage patterns that do not mirror the patterns that were taught.

There Are Predictable Sequences in SLA Such That Certain Structures Have To Be Acquired Before Others Can Be Integrated

This generalization is related to the previous one about how learners create a systematic interlanguage. There is evidence in SLA research to support that L2 learners acquire various grammatical features in predictable orders and over extensive amounts of time. Certain features of an L2 have to be acquired before other features can be integrated into the developing system. Evidence for these predictable sequences can be found in what are called stages of development. **Stages of development** refer to how a learner acquires a particular linguistic feature of an L2 over time. One well-documented example of this involves the acquisition of negation in English. The following displays the types of structures that learners produce as they pass through each stage (taken from Ellis, 1986, pp. 59–60).

Stage 1: no + PHRASE

No drink.

No you playing here.

Stage 2: negator moves inside phrase; *not* and *don't* added to list of negators, but *don't* is considered one word

I no can swim.

I don't see nothing mop.

Stage 3: negator attached to modals but initially may be unanalyzed as is *don't* in Stage 2

I can't play this one.

I won't tell.

Stage 4: auxiliary system of English is developed, and learner acquires correct use of *not* and contractions.

He doesn't know anything.

I didn't say it.

These stages for the acquisition of negation in English show that learners make particular kinds of errors as they reach different stages in the acquisition of a particular structure regardless of what their L1 is. As they pass through each stage, some kind of restructuring happens in the learners' linguistic system for that particular structure.

Another example can be found in what are called acquisition orders. **Acquisition orders** refer to the sequential order in which L2 learners acquire various grammatical features (as opposed to a specific grammatical feature as is the case with developmental stages) over time. Research shows that learners acquire certain grammatical features in predictable orders regardless of the order in which they were formally taught in the classroom. In English, the following order has been documented for the acquisition of verb morphemes:

1. *-ing*
2. regular past tense
3. irregular past tense
4. third-person present tense *-s*

If we examined speech from L2 English learners, we would see that regardless of what their L1 is, they will master the use of *-ing* first, followed by the regular past tense, then the irregular past tense and finally the third-person present *-s*. This order would appear even if learners were formally taught third-person present tense *-s* first. Acquisition orders have also been observed for other languages such as French, Spanish and German.

Acquisition orders and developmental stages appear to be impermeable to instruction and other outside influences because learners of all types will make the same type of errors in the same order no matter what kind of formal instruction they receive. These orders are universal. No matter how instructors teach certain structures or how much they get their learners to practice the forms, or how much error correction is used, they will not be able to alter these orders.

Researchers often refer to acquisition orders and developmental stages as empirical evidence to support that learners have "internal strategies" for organizing language data (Corder, 1981; Lee & VanPatten, 2003). Krashen (discussed in Chapter 1), for example, relied on this research to make his case that formal instruction has no role to play in acquisition.

> ## Pause to consider . . .
>
> the research on stages of development and acquisition orders. How might L2 instructors use this area of research in SLA to inform their teaching? Hint: The answer is NOT so that they can plan their syllabus according to these universal orders. Why is this not feasible?

Practice Does Not Make Perfect

This generalization is also related to the two previous ones. Because interlanguage development is systematic and learners follow universal developmental sequences that are impermeable to formal instruction, no amount of practice will make learners acquire what they are not ready to. Lightbown (1985) points out that when learners are given extensive practice with a particular form, they may exhibit high levels of accuracy with that form for a given period of time but this accuracy will eventually drop because learners will either forget the form or overgeneralize the use of the form. When learners are developmentally ready to acquire the form, accuracy levels for that form will rise again. Researchers sometimes refer to this phenomenon as "U-shaped development."

Knowing a Language Rule Does Not Mean One Will Be Able to Use It in Communicative Interaction

As L2 instructors, we can all probably relate to this generalization. How many times have we seen our students use a rule correctly on a test but then fail to use the same linguistic structure correctly in spontaneous conversation? As you may recall from our discussion in Chapter 1, Krashen (1982) attributes this phenomenon to the distinction he makes between "acquisition" and "learning." According to Krashen, metalinguistic information does not have any direct impact on "acquired" implicit knowledge.

The extent to which explicit knowledge may impact "acquisition" as defined by Krashen remains debatable in SLA research. Some researchers such as Ellis (1993) and Lightbown (1998), however, have suggested that explicit knowledge could help heighten learners' awareness of certain structures so that they may acquire them faster when they are developmentally ready to.

Isolated Explicit Error Correction Is Usually Ineffective in Changing Language Behavior

This generalization is related to the fact that interlanguage behavior is systematic and impermeable to the effects of formal instruction. Telling learners that they have made an error will not alter their interlanguage behavior so that the error will not be made again. Research in SLA suggests that in order for error correction to be effective, it must be carried out over sustained periods of time, and it must be focused on forms that learners are developmentally ready to learn.

For Most Adult Learners, Acquisition Stops Before the Learner Has Achieved Native-Like Mastery of the Target Language

No matter how much time and effort L2 learners devote to learning an L2, most will never become native-like. Their implicit linguistic system and/or their ability to use their linguistic system tend to remain nonnative-like. Even those very advanced learners who have spent extensive periods abroad interacting in the L2 will often still speak with an accent, no matter how fluent or accurate they are with other aspects of the language. For others, they may still struggle with using certain prepositions or idiomatic features of the L2 correctly.

It is not clear why L2 learners rarely become native-like. Some researchers have proposed that there may be a **critical period** for language acquisition, that is to say, a period in human development where SLA becomes more difficult. This critical period is believed to be around the age of puberty. If learners begin SLA after the critical period, they may have a more difficult time learning the L2 and will most probably never become native-like. However, there are other researchers who do not believe that there is a critical period for SLA. According to these researchers, nonnativeness may be a result of how much input the learner receives over time. In other words, those who start learning an L2 early may do better not because there is a critical period but because they will have had more opportunities to receive input over the course of their lifetime than those who start L2 learning later. These different positions are summarized in Birdsong (1999) as well as in Harley and Wang (1997).

Pause to consider . . .

the idea of a critical period. Do you think there is a critical period for learning skills like playing a musical instrument, sports or chess?

One Cannot Achieve Native-Like (Or Near Native-Like) Command of a Second Language in One Hour a Day (Over Two Years)

It is not clear how much time it takes, but it is certain that native or near native-like competence cannot be achieved exclusively in the classroom no matter how hard students work and no matter how talented the instructors are. Thus, it is highly unrealistic to expect students to be near native-like after going through a typical two-year basic language instruction program. Lightbown (1985) notes that the most successful language learners have been estimated to have spent some 12,000 to 15,000 hours "acquiring" the L2 by the age of six. Furthermore, learners in French immersion programs have been estimated to have received about 4,000 hours of contact with French by Grade 6. As Lightbown points out, in most school programs, the total number of hours after six years of language study for approximately five hours a week would not even reach 1,000.

Pause to consider . . .

the fact that native-like competence cannot be achieved in the classroom in one hour a day. How might teachers use this generalization about SLA to inform their teaching practices?

The Learner's Task Is Enormous Because Language Is Enormously Complex

We say that the learner's task is enormous and that language is complex because learning an L2 entails acquiring many aspects of the target language (e.g., the lexicon, the phonological system, syntax, pragmatics, etc) and in most cases, all these things must happen at the same time. In addition to *what* L2 learners must learn, there is also the question of *how* acquisition happens. VanPatten (2003) identifies at least three processes that are involved in SLA. These processes include **input processing, system change** and **output processing**. We will discuss these processes in more detail in Chapter 3.

Learners' Ability to Understand Language in a Meaningful Context Exceeds Their Ability to Comprehend Decontextualized Language and To Produce Language of Comparable Complexity and Accuracy

We have all observed this phenomenon in our own classrooms. Relying on context and background knowledge, L2 learners may be able to comprehend the language they hear even if they do not understand the forms that encode the meaning or be able to produce the forms accurately. Currently, the relationship between comprehension and production is not entirely clear but there is ample evidence to show that comprehension often precedes production. The explanation may be in part due to the developmental sequences that we discussed earlier. That is to say, while learners may not be developmentally ready to acquire various formal features of the L2, they may be able to extract meaning using contextual cues and world knowledge.

To summarize, this section has defined acquisition in terms of a series of generalizations about SLA made by Lightbown (1985, 2000). Similar statements have also been made by other researchers such as Lee and VanPatten's (2003) "five givens about SLA," and Long's (1990) essay on "The Least a Theory of SLA Needs to Explain." These generalizations should help us understand the nature of acquisition better and, consequently, help us have better and more realistic expectations about how L2 instruction may (or may not) enhance SLA.

Why SLA Theory and Research? What Is Their Relationship to Real-World Teaching?

In Chapter 1, we saw the birth and decline of a number of teaching methods over the course of history. This continues to happen today. Every now and then, a method or textbook that purports to embrace a new teaching approach will make its debut in the parade of foreign teaching methodologies. With so many teaching methods and instructional materials to choose from, each claiming to be new and improved, how is a language instructor supposed to choose?

Frustrated by the overwhelming number of methods, some may opt not to adhere to any particular teaching approach at all. I've heard some instructors say that they use an eclectic approach, that is to say, they take bits and pieces from various methods to suit their daily teaching needs guided by practical experience and intuition. Practical experience and intuition are certainly important factors but they are not enough on their own. In order to adequately evaluate new or existing approaches and materials, instructors need to have at least a working knowledge of SLA theory and the research evidence that exists to support this theory. Here are some reasons why.

Effective Teaching Practices Are Informed by SLA

When teachers understand how people acquire new languages, they will be in a better position to design or adopt (or pick and choose in an eclectic fashion) various instructional practices to enable their students to become as successful as they can as language learners. When teachers understand that input and interaction are essential ingredients to SLA, they will make sure that their students have ample opportunities to receive and interact with input. They will not spend the majority of their class time doing pattern drills. As stated in a previous publication (Wong, 2002a), teaching an L2 without an understanding of how learners acquire languages is like a doctor practicing medicine without an understanding of how the human body works. The better teachers understand how SLA works, the better they will be able to teach their students.

Instructional Materials Do Not Always Reflect SLA Theory or Research

Instructors need to be cautious about what commercial instructional materials claim to offer. Lightbown (2000) points out that "some aspects of SLA research and theory have become so completely integrated into mainstream FL/SL pedagogy that they are referred to without reference to their sources" (p. 438). There are textbooks that do indeed reflect current developments in SLA theory and research. However, the unfortunate reality is that some commercial materials on the market do not, even when they claim to. In my experience with reviewing foreign language textbooks, I have observed that some of the so called communicative textbooks hardly contain any activities that encourage learners to engage in interpreting and negotiating meaning. Musumeci (1997) corroborates these observations when she reports an example from a proposal for a new language textbook in which "communicative activities" were reduced to meaning any kind of pair or group work (p. 130). Taking this misguided line of logic, a new instructor may inaccurately think that a pattern drill is a communicative activity if students worked on the drill in pairs. I will cite one further example. I was recently asked to evaluate the proposal for a first-year French textbook that was supposed to be content-based, the content being commercial French. As you may recall from Chapter 1, in content-based instruction, the L2 is used as the medium of communication (as opposed to the object of study) for subject matter learning. Excited at the prospect of such a book (as first-year content-based textbooks in French are infrequent), I agreed to review it. However, when I evaluated the sample chapters, I discovered that this was far from being a content-based textbook. The chapters primarily consisted of detailed grammatical explanations followed by mechanical drills that were contextualized with commercial French vocabulary. The authors and editors, evidently, had a very different idea about what content-based instruction was. Why this mismatch between theory, approach and instructional materials? One reason is that not all textbook editors and authors may be familiar with research in SLA. Often, authors write textbooks based on their own intuitions about how languages are learned, usually drawing on their own language-learning experiences. "This is how I learned language so it must work." There are, of course, textbooks out there that are indeed based on sound theoretical principles. The point here is that unless instructors have some understanding of SLA theory and research, they will not be able to judge the validity of what different instructional materials claim to offer. Therefore, being informed about research in SLA provides us with the best tool for evaluating various theories, teaching practices, and beliefs about language instruction. As Musumeci (1997) pointed out, teaching methodology is only useful and important "to the extent that teachers understand the principles" underlying it (p. 128).

Pause to consider . . .

the mismatch between theory and practice. Can you think of examples in L2 instruction or in other fields where theory is mistranslated into practice?

SLA Offers Realistic Expectations about Teaching and Learning

Understanding the nature of SLA also helps instructors have realistic expectations about their students and about themselves as teachers. Instructors tend to become frustrated when their students make certain errors over and over again after they have explained the concept repeatedly. Is this due to poor teaching? Does this mean that the students are lazy? Not necessarily. Instructors need to understand that SLA is constrained by a variety of factors. As we saw earlier in our discussion about the nature of acquisition based on Lightbown's statements, SLA is highly complex and slow, and the reality is that most L2 learners do not reach native-like competence. Therefore, it is important to keep in mind that the lack of immediate results does not necessarily mean that teachers or students were not doing their jobs. When teachers have a better understanding of the complex nature of SLA, their expectations of learners will also be more realistic and they will be in a better position to assess the outcomes of their own teaching.

Pause to consider . . .

the nature of SLA and assessment in the classroom. Given what we know about the complex nature of SLA, instructors should expect learners to make certain kinds of errors. How do you think these errors should be treated or corrected in exam situations such as oral exams or the composition components of tests?

How Should Instructors Approach the Application of SLA Research?

In this chapter, I have discussed the nature of SLA and outlined why it is important for L2 instructors to have a working knowledge of SLA theory and research to guide their instructional decisions. It is also necessary to point out, however, that this does not mean that research results in SLA can always be directly applied to classroom instruction. First, as discussed earlier, research experiments in SLA are not designed to answer the day-to-day questions about effective language teaching. Second, the contexts in which research experiments are conducted do not always make research results directly applicable to local classroom conditions. In research experiments on instructional effects, researchers must isolate the effects of different variables. In order to do this, they may need to administer instructional treatments to subjects that teachers would not normally do in an actual classroom learning setting. For example, I recently conducted an experiment on a type of instruction called Processing Instruction (Wong, 2004b). This type of instruction includes a combination of explicit information about a target form followed by structured input practice activities (see Chapter 6). In order to isolate the individual effects of the explicit information and practice activities, I used four different groups of subjects in my study: I gave one group of subjects both the explicit information and the structured input activities, I gave a second group only the structured input activities, I gave a third group only the explicit information, and I gave a fourth group no instruction at all (control group). In a classroom learning context, would it be feasible to only give students explicit information (or no instruc-tion) and then test them on the target forms without engaging them in any kind of practice? The answer is, of course, no. However, in order for me to see whether explicit information was doing anything at all in the context of my research, I had to isolate the effect of this variable by giving one group of subjects only the explicit information. Therefore, what is necessary for researchers to do in the context of research does not always reflect what is best for classroom learning contexts.

Pause to consider . . .

the study I just described. My results revealed that explicit information was not necessary for the subjects to make statistical gains on paper-and-pencil posttests. Does this mean that instructors should never use explicit information in the classroom? Explain.

The particular subjects used in a study and the specific learning contexts of a research experiment also may not reflect the local conditions of instructors' individual classrooms. Let's imagine that we have a study about how inter-national students in an intensive English class at an American university acquire question forms. How should an instructor who teaches English to adult immigrants at a community center in Québec use these research results? What about an instructor in Hong Kong who teaches English to fifth graders twice a week? Direct application of research results is obviously not the answer here. Instructors may certainly gain some valuable insight from this study as to what factors may impact the acquisition of question forms in English, but much thought and interpretation will be needed before they can consider applying the research results to their local classroom conditions. Here are some points and questions to keep in mind when reading and interpreting research reports:

- *Age of Subjects:* Would the results of the study be the same or different with learners of a different age?
- *Target Structure:* Would the results of the study be the same of different if a different target structure were used?
- *Assessment Measures:* Would the results of the study be the same or different if different assessment measures were used? Might we get different results if we used an oral picture description task instead of a discrete point pencil and paper task?
- *Level of Learners:* Might we get different results if we repeated the study with advanced learners rather than with beginning learners, for example?
- *Number of Instructional Contact Hours:* How might research results be different if the study were conducted in an immersion context where students have 30 hours of target language instruction a week versus a learning context where students only have 4–5 hours of target language instruction per week?

All these factors may have an impact on the results of any given SLA study. Thus, as you read the SLA research presented in subsequent chapters, you should keep these questions in mind when you try to interpret the results.

To reiterate, SLA research is an important source of information to help instructors make sound pedagogical decisions. While the details of research experiments may not be directly applicable to day-to-day classroom instruction, instructors should gain valuable insight from this research about the nature of SLA to help them develop effective teaching principles.

Pause to consider . . .

the interpretation of research findings. Besides age, target structure, assessment measures, level of learners, and instructional contact hours, can you think of other factors that may have an impact on research results?

SUMMARY/CONCLUSION

We have seen that SLA research provides valuable information about how languages are acquired and the different factors that may impact the effectiveness of different instructional interventions. Instructors who are knowledgeable about research in SLA will be better equipped to evaluate existing and new teaching approaches and techniques. They will be better teachers because they will have more realistic expectations for themselves and their students and will be able to understand the needs of their learners better. We also pointed out that while SLA research should be used by instructors to guide their pedagogical decisions, this research must also be interpreted with caution. Research contexts do not always reflect classroom learning conditions and consequently, research results may not be directly applicable to local classroom learning situations. For this reason, instructors need to carefully consider the differences between the context in which the research study was conducted and the specific context of their individual classrooms and learners. SLA research is indeed an important knowledge source to inform our pedagogical choices but as Lightbown pointed out, "it is not the details of the individual studies that can be 'applied' but rather the general principles which they reflect" (Lightbown, 2000, p. 454). In the next chapter, we will focus on the nature of input, an essential ingredient of SLA, so that we may better understand and appreciate the instructional techniques put forth by this book—input enhancement techniques.

ENHANCE YOUR KNOWLEDGE

SLA Research and Classroom Practice

Musumeci, D. (1997). *Breaking tradition.* New York: McGraw-Hill.
Lightbown, P. (1985). Great expectations: Second-language acquisition research and classroom teaching. *Applied Linguistics, 6,* 173–189.
Lightbown, P. (2000). Classroom SLA research and second language teaching. *Applied Linguistics, 21,* 431–462.

CHAPTER 3

Input and Input Enhancement

Before discussing the different input enhancement techniques in this book and how they may be used to enhance SLA, it is first important to understand what input is and the role it plays in SLA. What is input? You have already seen this term used in the first two chapters. We will now discuss this concept in detail.

WHAT IS INPUT?

In the context of language acquisition, **input** refers to samples of language that learners are exposed to in a communicative context or setting. It is language that has some kind of communicative intent, that is to say, that there is a message to be communicated in the utterance so that the receiver of the message has a reason for attending to it. Researchers such as Schwartz call this type of meaning-bearing input **primary linguistic data** (Schwartz, 1993). **Input** or **primary linguistic data** is language that contains instances or exemplars of various grammatical forms and other linguistic information in the language environment of the language acquirer (Schwartz, 1993).

In the context of L1 acquisition, children are bombarded by input in their environment. "Do you want a drink of water? Don't forget to wash before dinner. Make sure you eat all your vegetables." These are all examples of input that a child may hear. People learning an L2 also receive input. Immigrants and language learners studying abroad, for example, are surrounded by L2 input as they go about their daily routines. At the bank, they may hear, "Could you please fill out this deposit slip." At the supermarket, they may be asked "Do you prefer paper or plastic?" by the person bagging groceries. Input may also be written. Billboards along the highway and advertisements or signs on a bus all constitute sources of input.

L2 learners in a foreign-language-learning context also get input. When learners hear "Please open your books to page 78" or "Please get into groups of three" in the target language, they are receiving input. Other sources of input may come from watching a film, listening to a song, looking at advertisements or magazines and interacting with the instructor and other students in the L2. These examples illustrate that language learners may get input from an endless variety of sources. What is common to all these examples is that the language they hear or read contains a message that has to be comprehended. Input, then, is necessarily meaning-bearing for it communicates some kind of message. When a language learner hears "Paper or plastic?", someone is communicating something. When a language learner sees a sign that reads "Bathroom Out of Order", a message is also communicated. The learner's job is to receive and understand these messages.

Another characteristic of input that is important for language acquisition is that it must also somehow be **comprehensible.** If input involves the communication of a message, the learner must somehow be able to extract the meaning of the message. This does not mean that learners need to understand every word of the message but they should be able to make sense of the message in some way. Input that is completely incomprehensible will not be of much use to learners.

Interactional and Non-Interactional Input

Ellis (1994) makes a distinction between two types of input for acquisition: interactional and noninteractional input. **Interactional input** is input that is received in the context of interaction where there is some kind of communicative exchange involving the learner and at least one other person. A learner may be conversing with a native speaker, another learner or an instructor. Playing games, conversations with friends and family and classroom interactions all constitute examples of interactional input. **Non-interactional input,** on the other hand, occurs in the context of non-reciprocal discourse (Ellis, 1994). Learners in this case are not part of the interaction. Listening to announcements on the subway, watching television, listening to the radio or attending class lectures are all examples of non-interactional input.

Both interactional and non-interactional language can provide rich sources of input for language learners. However, in the case of interactional input, learners have the added advantage of being able to negotiate meaning, that is to say, they can let their interlocutors know if they do not understand what is said and ask for clarification. This renders the input more comprehensible and more accessible for acquisition. This is one of the reasons why interaction is also considered to be important for SLA (Gass, 1997).

Pause to consider . . .

incomprehensible input. Can you remember situations where the L2 input that you heard was not comprehensible? What factors contributed to making the input difficult to comprehend?

What Input Is NOT

In order to better understand the nature of input, it is helpful to also know what input is *not*. Input is meaning-bearing language that learners hear or see. It is not language that learners produce. Language that is produced is called **output.** Of course, if someone is producing meaning-bearing language, that person's output could become input for someone else.

Explicit information *about* language is also not input for acquisition. Pedagogical grammar rules and explanations about grammar points are not input because they do not constitute meaning-bearing language in the sense that there is a communicative message the learner is supposed to attend to. *Il faut manger votre repas lentement* (You must eat your meal slowly) said by a teacher to a student in the cafeteria is meaning-bearing input for acquisition because there is a message being communicated here. "Adverbs in French are formed by adding *-ment* to adjectives that end in an *-e*" is not input for acquisition.

Now what if the explicit information were given in the target language? Would that be input? When instructors are explaining the rules for a particular grammatical form in the L2, they are communicating a message to students and in that sense, we can say that meaning-bearing input is involved. However, this explicit information is qualitatively different from the kind of primary linguistic data that is essential for creating a new implicit linguistic system. For example, let's say an instructor wants ESL (English as a Second Language) students to learn past tense formation in English. The explicit information provided to students in English (the L2 in this case) may be something like the following: "To form the past tense in English, you need to add *-ed* to regular verbs." A message is being communicated here in the target language but notice that this utterance does not contain *input* in the past tense. In other words, this utterance does not contain instances or examples of the past tense being used. Learners are learning information about how the past tense is formed but they are not necessarily getting input that contains uses of the past tense. The explicit information only speaks about the past tense as a topic. Thus, unless the instructor is also using the target structure (the past tense in this case) while giving the explanation, it is not linguistic input with regard to that structure.[1] In this book, I use the term **input** to refer to primary linguistic data that contain exemplars of particular target linguistic information used in a communicative context.

Pause to consider . . .

the nature of input. Which of the following examples is an example of input for acquisition as used in this book?

1. My brother loves animals. He has many pets. He has three birds, two cats, two dogs and three turtles. He is thinking of buying two ferrets next week.
2. To make a noun plural in English, you must add an *-s* to the end of the noun.

How are these two examples different from each other?

I would like to clarify that I do not mean to say that information about language cannot be useful for language acquisition (a point we will discuss in greater detail in subsequent sections). The point I want to make is that explicit information about language does not represent the kind of primary linguistic data that learners need to construct an implicit linguistic system. Without such data, instruction is pointless.

What Is the Role of Input in SLA?

We have already discussed that SLA is a complex process that involves the creation of an implicit (unconscious) linguistic system. Input provides the linguistic data that a developing linguistic system needs in order for acquisition to be possible. When learners receive input, they are feeding their developing linguistic system the data it needs to start the process of acquisition. Without input, successful language acquisition cannot happen. All scholars in SLA are in agreement that input is fundamental to language acquisition. Here is what one scholar has to say: "The concept of input is perhaps the single most important concept of second language acquisition. It is trivial to point out that no individual can learn a second language without input of some sort" (Gass, 1997, p. 1). There are no cases of successful learners who have not been exposed to lots of input. Learners who have mastered their L2 usually read a lot in the L2, listen to music and watch TV in the L2, have friends who speak the L2, and so on. Input is like fuel for a car or a plane. Without fuel, these machines cannot run. Without input, there can be no successful language acquisition.

How Do Learners Get Linguistic Data from Input?

As discussed earlier, learners are exposed to input whenever they hear or see language that contains a message to be communicated. Thus, the amount of input they are exposed to could be vast. Unfortunately, all the input that learners are exposed to is not necessarily viable for acquisition. Because it is not possible to pay attention to everything in the environment, learners cannot take in all the input that they are exposed to. Input, then, is somehow filtered by the internal mechanisms of learners. How does this happen?

Many scholars in SLA agree that in order for input to be usable for acquisition, it must be *noticed* or attended to in some way (e.g., Gass, 1997; VanPatten, 1996; Wong & Simard, 2001). What do we mean by "attending" to input? Currently, SLA researchers are not all in agreement as to what attending to input entails. Schmidt (1990, 1993, 1995, 2001) postulates that only features of input that have been consciously noticed by learners are usable for acquisition. Other researchers say that input must be "detected" but that this detection does not have to involve conscious awareness (Tomlin & Villa, 1994). Because it is quite tricky to measure the construct of awareness in experimental research, it has been difficult to find empirical support for either position. Nevertheless, regardless of the position researchers may take regarding the issue of awareness, there is a general consensus along with support from SLA research that some form of attention to input is necessary in order for input to be usable for SLA (Wong, 2001). Research has shown that in some cases, greater degrees of attention (which may or may not involve awareness) may lead to more learning (e.g., Huot, 1995; Leow, 1998, Rosa & O'Neill, 1999). In this book, when we say that input must be noticed, we mean that the learner has paid attention to it. This attention may or may not involve conscious awareness. In the next section, we will see what happens to L2 input once it does get noticed.

> ## *Pause to consider . . .*
>
> the construct of awareness in SLA research. Why do you suppose it is so difficult to measure the construct of awareness in experimental research?

VanPatten's (1996) Model of SLA

We mentioned earlier that SLA involves at least three sets of processes. These processes are depicted in Figure 3.1.

In this model of SLA by VanPatten, when learners attend to or notice input and comprehend the message, a **form-meaning connection** is made. **Form,** used in this sense, refers to surface features of language such as verbal and nominal morphology and functional items of language like prepositions, articles and pronouns (VanPatten, 1996). "Form" could also be used at the word level to refer to word form (Barcroft, 2000). For example, all words have form and a referent. In the word *boy,* the form of the word is the letters *b-o-y*. The referent is the meaning of the word, that is to say, "a young human being who is male." **Meaning,** therefore, refers to referential real-world meaning. A **form-meaning connection** is the relationship between referential meaning and the way it is encoded linguistically. When L2 learners hear the word *boy* and understands that it means a young male that has not yet reached adulthood, a form-meaning connection is made. When learners hear *I talked to my professor* and understand that *talked* means that the action is in

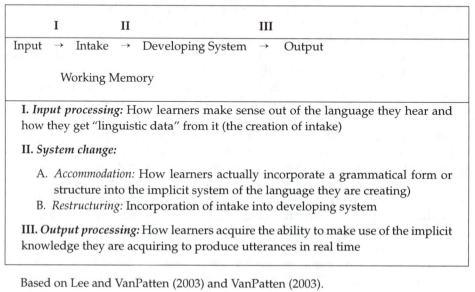

Based on Lee and VanPatten (2003) and VanPatten (2003).

FIGURE 3.1 Three sets of processes in second language acquisition

the past, or if they hear *Sylvie regardera un film* (Sylvie will watch a film) and understand that *regardera* refers to the future, another form-meaning connection is made.

It is important to point out here that in order to make form-meaning connections, it is not enough that learners just notice the form. Noticing a form is a start but in order to make form-meaning connections, they also need to comprehend the meaning that the form encodes. For example, a learner of French may notice the plural marker *-aux* of the noun *hôpitaux* in the sentence *Les hôpitaux dans mon quartier sont excellents* (The hospitals in my neighborhood are excellent), but not understand that *-aux* encodes the meaning of plurality. In this case, we say that the learner has noticed the form but has not made a form-meaning connection. Of course with subsequent exposure to and noticing of the form over time, the learner may eventually also comprehend the meaning of the form and make a form-meaning connection. To reiterate, in order to make form-meaning connections, learners need to both *notice* the form and *comprehend* the meaning that the form encodes.

Form-meaning connections, also known as **intake,** have the potential to be internalized. The process in SLA that is involved in converting input into intake is called **input processing.** As you can see in Figure 3.1, acquisition begins with exposure to input. When learners attend to input and make form-meaning connections, that input becomes intake. Thus, only a subset of input becomes intake. This intake is held in working memory and has the potential to be internalized. When this happens, the developing linguistic system must make room for or accommodate this new linguistic data (i.e., through a form-meaning connection). Once a new form-meaning connection has been accommodated, the developing system changes and is restructured. The process that entails accommodation of intake data into the developing system and restructuring of that system is called **system change.** This process may be partial or incomplete. For reasons that we do not quite understand, some linguistic forms may be incorporated and some may not. Finally, linguistic data that have been incorporated into the developing system may be eventually accessed by the learner as output or production. This process is called **output processing.**

SLA, then, is directly dependent on intake and not on input since only intake data is usable for acquisition. The more intake that is created, the better acquisition will be. The model also shows that SLA is not dependent on output. Output is language that learners produce. Output is not possible unless there is good input and intake. Of course learners may be able to repeat verbatim what a teacher says or give answers to a mechanical drill without receiving any input, but the language that is produced here is not output in the sense that the learner is able to access language that has been internalized by their developing linguistic systems; it is mere repetition. Therefore, the richer the input in the learners' environment, the better the potential for intake.

Gass's (1997) Model of SLA

Gass (1997) proposed a model that includes three stages to account for the conversion of input to intake.

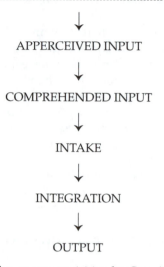

INPUT

- -

↓

APPERCEIVED INPUT

↓

COMPREHENDED INPUT

↓

INTAKE

↓

INTEGRATION

↓

OUTPUT

FIGURE 3.2 Model of second language acquisition by Gass (1997)

The dotted line underneath input serves to illustrate that input is filtered by the internal mechanisms of learners. Some language data will filter through, some will not. The first stage, **apperception,** entails that the learners must recognize that there is something out there to be learned. **Apperceived input** is input that has been noticed in some way by the learner and functions as a priming device that prepares the input for further analysis (Gass, 1997, p. 4). Like in VanPatten's model, Gass' model also shows that in order for apperceived input to become intake, input must be comprehended. Comprehension of input entails that the learner analyzes the input in some way to extract meaning. Gass (1997) offers consonant length in Italian as an example. In Italian, consonant length can serve to differentiate between different meanings of words: *capelli* (hair) versus *cappelli* (hats). The learner must first recognize this phenomenon, that is to say, that different consonant lengths in Italian can affect the meaning of words. This is the apperception stage. Comprehension kicks in and intake is created when the learner also recognizes the difference between *capelli* and *cappelli* and connects the concept "hair" to the form *capelli* and the concept "hats" to the form *cappelli*.

Learners Must Receive, Notice, and Comprehend Input

Both VanPatten's and Gass's models illustrate the necessity for learners to receive, comprehend, and notice input. Both models underscore the importance of comprehension in SLA and by extension, why input needs to be comprehensible. Input is fundamental for acquisition because it provides the data that is available for intake. However, if learners do not notice and comprehend the input, form-meaning connections or intake will not be created and that input will have little use for acquisition.

Is Exposure to Input Sufficient?

It should be clear by now that input is a crucial ingredient for language acquisition. As you may recall in Chapter 1, Krashen has gone as far as to posit that exposure to comprehensible input alone is sufficient for SLA. According to Krashen, if learners have access to an optimal amount of comprehensible input, then acquisition should just happen naturally. Pointing to research on developmental stages and acquisition orders, he claims that formal instruction has no use for acquisition.

Krashen is certainly correct to point out that SLA cannot take place without lots of comprehensible input. It is also true that people can and do learn L2s in the absence of any kind of formal instruction. Consider, for example, the diaries and records of Marco Polo and the missionaries who came to the New World (Wong & VanPatten, 2003). However, when efficiency and accuracy are at stake, learning an L2 via comprehensible input alone may not be the best option. Here are some reasons why.

First, as we saw in Chapter 1, input tends not to be as abundant as we would like in many L2 classrooms. Wing (1987) found that the average L2 instructor used the target language only about 50% of the time. Of that 50%, only about half of that language was actually communicative in nature. This means that in the average L2 classroom, only about 25% of teacher talk could be considered input for acquisition. Second, even when input may be abundant, such as is the case with learners in immersion programs, learners do not always notice or attend to certain features of input on their own. Recall from the previous section that in order for input to be usable for language acquisition, learners must attend to it in some way and make form-meaning connections. Research has also found that even when learners do attend to input, they may not always make the correct form-meaning connections (e.g., VanPatten & Cadierno, 1993; VanPatten & Wong, 2004). Spanish, for example, has flexible word order and does not always follow a subject-verb-object order. Therefore, it is not uncommon to find object-verb-subject word orders in Spanish. VanPatten and Cadierno (1993) found that L2 Spanish learners have a tendency to incorrectly think that the first noun they hear in utterances is always the agent (or person performing the action). Even though these learners paid attention to direct object pronouns, they were not making the correct form-meaning connection. What these examples suggest is that while input is a necessary ingredient for SLA, mere exposure to input may not be enough for many learning contexts. Sometimes input may need to be enhanced via some kind of formal instruction to help learners attend to it.

Does Instruction Make a Difference?

We need to keep two things in mind when addressing the potential effects of instruction. These are (a) the rate of acquisition and (b) the route of acquisition. **Rate of acquisition** refers to the speed in which learners acquire certain features of an L2. The order in which they do so is the **route of acquisition.** The research evidence for the existence of acquisitional orders and developmental stages suggests that instruction cannot alter the route of acquisition. As was discussed earlier, research shows that learners acquire certain grammatical features in predictable orders regardless of the order in which they were formally taught in the classroom. After years of accumulated research in this area, most scholars in SLA are in agreement that formal instruction cannot change the order in which certain grammatical features are acquired (e.g., Ellis, 1989, 1994; Larsen-Freeman & Long, 1990; Lightbown, 1983; Long, 1988, etc.). Ellis (1994) found, for example, that classroom ESL learners who received formal instruction and practice in grammar displayed the same developmental stages as nonclassroom learners for the acquisition of English negation as well as other structures. Kaplan (1987) reported similar findings with learners of French in the United States for the acquisition of the *passé composé* (past tense) and the *imparfait* (imperfect) in French. What these and other studies suggest is that learners have internal mechanisms that guide SLA and that these mechanisms do not appear to be permeable to instruction.

You may be asking at this point, "So is there any point to teaching at all?" The answer is yes. While instruction does not appear to affect the order of acquisition, it does appear to affect the rate of acquisition. In other words, formal instruction may speed up the acquisition of certain features of an L2. Overall, research that compares classroom learning with naturalistic learning suggests that learners who have some kind of formal instruction learn certain features more quickly and as a result may go further down the path of acquisition (see Long, 1983, and Doughty, 2003, for reviews of research on the effects of instruction). Why is this?

First, classroom learners tend to be exposed to richer and more complex input than those in a lot of "naturalistic" environments such as those that immigrants tend to find themselves in. In many ethnic communities such as Chinatown in Chicago, L2 input tends to be limited to conversational language. In the classroom, however, learners tend to be exposed to both conversational language and planned discourse in the form of authentic written texts and formal speeches among other sources. As Lee and VanPatten (2003) point out, the input in planned discourse tends to be richer and more complex, contain a larger range of grammatical structures, more complex syntax and broader vocabulary. Thus, in the classroom, instructors can deliberately expose learners to richer input.

Second, formal instruction may heighten learners' awareness of things in the input they might miss otherwise or might get wrong (e.g., make the wrong form-meaning connection). Recall that only input that learners attend to or notice in some way has the potential to affect acquisition. Therefore, formal instruction could be used to make certain forms in input more salient so learners might notice and perhaps process them more quickly.

Why Input Enhancement?

The realization that input is not always abundant in L2 classrooms and the finding that learners do not always pay attention to what they need to in the input have prompted the language teaching profession to seek instructional techniques to make SLA better and more efficient. Input enhancement, a concept first introduced by Sharwood Smith, represents one viable option to do this. As you may recall from Chapter 1, Sharwood Smith defines **input enhancement** as any pedagogical intervention that is used to make specific features of L2 input more salient as an effort to draw learners' attention to these features. Input enhancement is based on the undisputed position in SLA that comprehensible input is crucial to acquisition and the position that only input that learners attend to or notice in some way can have an impact on acquisition. Among the examples that Sharwood Smith offered as input enhancement techniques in his original discussion are input flood (see Chapter 4), typographically enhancing target linguistic features, and providing learners with metalinguistic rule explanations (1991, p. 119). The input enhancement techniques that this book focuses on are limited to those that draw on meaning-bearing primary linguistic data as their foundation for instruction. In other words, these techniques rely heavily on the provision of meaning-bearing input that contains exemplars of target forms. These techniques are input flood (Chapter 4), textual enhancement (Chapter 5), structured input (Chapter 6), and grammatical consciousness-raising tasks (Chapter 7).[2] While Sharwood Smith includes metalinguistic explanations as a form of input enhancement, this book does not treat this technique because it does not rely on primary linguistic data. This is not to say that I do not believe that such a technique can have value for SLA. I simply wish to point out that such a technique is fundamentally different from those that are input-based. I will discuss this in more detail in the next section.

What Can We Expect from Input Enhancement?

When examining these techniques, it is important to keep in mind that increasing the salience of input does not imply that the enhanced input will automatically become intake. Given the complex nature of SLA, it should be clear that instructors cannot control whether or not learners will process input correctly and efficiently, even when it is made salient. Sharwood Smith himself cautioned that while input enhancement is presumed to increase the chances that learners will attend to a target form, this does not mean that they will notice or internalize it. What these techniques *will* do is provide learners with supplementary doses of comprehensible input and boost the likelihood that they will notice what they need to in order to enhance the process of SLA.

We should also not expect learners to be able to immediately use the target forms accurately in production, even when they do notice forms. Remember that comprehension precedes production in SLA (Lightbown, 2000). Form-meaning connections need to be strengthened before they can be accessed for accurate production.

What about Explicit Information?

In the previous section, we saw that explicit information is not a pedagogical technique that relies on the provision of input in the sense that the input contains exemplars or uses of particular target forms. **Explicit information** is information about language, most often provided via pedagogical rules. Can explicit information have a positive impact on SLA?

First, it is important to keep in mind that instruction, no matter what form it may take, cannot alter the fundamental learning processes in SLA. With this constraint in mind, we may then ask, "Can explicit information enhance SLA by speeding up the process of acquisition?" To the extent that explicit information may help learners notice things in the input, it may have the potential to enhance SLA. When we explicitly tell learners about a form via rules or other explanations, learners may be primed to notice the form when it appears in a piece of input. Thus, like other input enhancement techniques, explicit information may help learners notice the forms faster. VanPatten (2004) adds that in addition to noticing, explanations may help learners understand the relationship between form and meaning (or function) more quickly, leading to increased comprehension. VanPatten points out that this may be particularly useful in contexts where temporal reference is not clear and learners must rely on verb forms alone to get meaning:

> . . . if I know that the past tense in a language is encoded with a
> stress shift from the stem of a verb to a final syllable and I know the
> shape of those final syllables, then I may be able to "comprehend"
> past tense more readily than if I didn't know this. To the extent that
> comprehension is a pre-requisite or part of acquisition (via some
> kind of input processing), any instruction that leads to increased
> comprehension may also lead to increased acquisition.
>
> —VanPatten, 2004

Thus, viewed in this light, explicit information may be beneficial in some cases. This does not mean, however, that class time should be devoted to explaining the L2. We must not forget that in order for any instructional technique to be effective, it must be provided via meaningful and communicative contexts. More importantly perhaps is the fact that explicit information cannot be a substitute for meaning-bearing input (i.e., primary linguistic data). We cannot ignore the fact that learners need access to abundant amounts of comprehensible input in order for acquisition to happen. In other words, instruction in the absence of input cannot lead to acquisition. Again, I am using input here to mean language that contains communicative uses of the target form. The drawback of explicit information, of course, is that it does not necessarily provide learners with additional amounts of input. Additionally, when instructors devote class time to explaining language, they are taking time away from providing students with input. Thus, one danger of explicit information is that it may rob learners of opportunities for exposure to input. Based on my observations of new teachers, I suspect that one of the reasons why explicit information is sometimes viewed in a negative light is because those who use it tend to use it abundantly. I have seen instructors get so caught up in explaining things that very little class time is left over for any kind of meaningful language use. The trick then becomes one of how to incorporate explicit information (if the decision is made to use it) into a lesson without denying learners the things we know are essential to SLA, that is to say, input and communicative use of language. Therefore, explicit information may be beneficial to the extent that it may help learners notice and comprehend L2 input better and more rapidly. Explicit information can, however, be detrimental to SLA if it robs learners of opportunities to receive comprehensible input and to engage in meaningful interaction.

SUMMARY/CONCLUSION

In this chapter, the nature of acquisition and the role of input in SLA were discussed in order to provide a theoretically sound rationale for the use of input enhancement. Input enhancement is based on the position in SLA that acquisition is input dependent and that learners must attend to input. A distinction was made between techniques that are input-based or rely on primary linguistic data (i.e., those presented in this book), and those that do not, that is to say, explicit information. Explicit information may help learners notice certain forms in input faster but it does not necessarily provide learners with additional input that contains communicative uses of a target form. Thus, should instructors decide to use explicit information, they need to make sure that opportunities for students to receive input and to engage in communicative interaction are not compromised. Input-based techniques, on the other hand, rely on primary linguistic data as their foundation for instruction. Thus, in addition to drawing learners' attention to form, these techniques have the added advantage of providing learners with additional doses of input. In the next chapters, we will turn our attention to these individual input enhancement techniques.

CHAPTER NOTES

1. Many scholars would agree that explicit information, even when it does contain exemplars of the target form, would not be the most useful source of "input" for beginning learners since they tend to lack the linguistic ability to process this information in the L2. Advanced learners would benefit more from this type of "input."
2. See Doughty and Williams (1998) Chapter 10 for a more comprehensive list of different types of instructional interventions (i.e., focus-on-form techniques).

ENHANCE YOUR KNOWLEDGE

More on the Givens of SLA

Long, M. H. (1990). The least a theory of second language acquisition must explain. *TESOL Quarterly, 24,* 649–666.

VanPatten, B. (2003). *From input to output: A teacher's guide to second language acquisition.* New York: McGraw Hill.

Acquisition Orders and Stages of Development

Bailey, N., Madden, C., & Krashen, S. D. (1974). Is there a natural sequence in adult second language learning? *Language Learning, 21,* 235–243.

Dulay, H., & Burt, M. (1974). Natural sequences in child second language acquisition. *Language Learning, 24,* 37–53.

Larsen-Freeman, D., & Long, M. (1991). *An introduction to second language acquisition.* New York: Longman. [See Chapter 4]

Non-Nativeness

Harley, B., & Wang, W. (1997). The critical period hypothesis: Where are we now? In A. M. B. de Groot & J. F. Kroll (Eds.), *Tutorials in bilingualism: Psycholinguistic perspectives* (pp. 19–51). Mahwah, NJ: Erlbaum.

Johnson, J. S. & Newport, E. (1989). Critical period effects in second language learning: The influence of maturational state on the acquisition of English as a second language. *Cognitive Psychology, 21*, 60–99.

Input

Krashen, S. D. (1985). *The Input Hypothesis: Issues and implications.* New York: Longman.

Lee, J. F. (2000). Five types of input and the various relationships between form and meaning. In J. Lee and A. Valdman (Eds.), *Form and meaning: Multiple perspectives* (pp. 25–42). AAUSC Issues in Language Program Direction, Boston: Heinle & Heinle.

Input and Interaction

Gass, S. M. (1997). *Input and interaction and the second language learner.* Mahwah, NJ: Erlbaum.

Input Processing

Klein, E. (1999). Just parsing through: notes on the state of L2 processing research today. In E. Klein & G. Martohardjono (Eds.) *The development of secondlLanguage grammars: A generative approach* (pp. 197–216). Philadelphia: Benjamins.

VanPatten, B. (1996). *Input processing and grammar instruction.* Norwood, NJ: Ablex.

Intake

Corder, P. (1967). The significance of learners' errors. *International Review of Applied Linguistics, 5*, 161–70. (reprinted in 1981)

VanPatten, B. (2000). Thirty years of input (or intake, the neglected sibling). In B. Swierzbin et. al. (Eds.), *Social and cognitive factors in second language acquisition* (pp. 287–311). Somerville, MA: Cascadilla Press.

Explicit Information

Ellis, N. (1994). *Implicit and explicit learning of languages.* London; San Diego: Academic Press.

DeKeyser, R. M. (1998). Beyond focus on form: Cognitive perspectives on learning and practicing second language grammar. In C. Doughty & J. Williams (Eds.), *Focus on form in classroom second language acquisition* (pp. 42–63). Cambridge: Cambridge University Press.

Schwartz, B. D. (1993). On explicit and negative data affecting competence and linguistic behavior. *Studies in Second Language Acquisition, 15*, 147–163.

Wong, W. (2004b). Processing instruction in French: The role of explicit information and structured input. In B. VanPatten (Ed.), *Processing instruction: Theory, research and commentary.* Mahwah, NJ: Erlbaum.

CHAPTER 4

Input Flood

WHAT IS INPUT FLOOD?

What does the word *flood* mean to you? Here are some sentences that contain the word *flood*.

The heavy rain resulted in a catastrophic flood in the area.

We were flooded with phone calls all day long.

When I returned from vacation, my e-mail account was flooded with junk mail.

There is a virtual flood of techniques dealing with grammar instruction.

As these examples illustrate, we use the word *flood* to mean "lots of" something. In language teaching, if we want our learners to notice a particular feature of the target language, we could flood the input with that particular linguistic feature. This technique is known as **input flood.**

In input flood, the input learners receive is saturated with the form that we hope learners will notice and possibly acquire. We don't usually highlight the form in any way to draw attention to it nor do we tell learners to pay attention to the form. We merely saturate the input with the form. The basic idea here is that by flooding the input with many exemplars of the form, learners will have an increased chance to notice it. Recall that in order for input to be usable for language acquisition, learners must attend to it or notice it in some way. Gass (1997) points out that the frequency of a particular target structure can have an impact on noticing. She explains that a target structure that appears frequently in input is more likely to be noticed by learners (p. 17).

How Is Input Flood Carried Out?

Input flood can be carried out with both written and oral input. In the written mode, input is modified so that many exemplars of the target form can be embedded in the instructional materials. A story or an article, for example, could be modified so that the target item can appear over and over again. In the oral mode, the target item could be embedded in natural speech or it could be embedded in written input and then read aloud to students. Sometimes we may find some authentic materials where there are already many instances of the form. In this case, very little (or no) modification may be necessary.

Pause to consider . . .

oral and written input. Do you think learners need both oral and written input? Do you think learners will notice forms more easily in oral input or written input? Why?

The following is an example of how an original text may be modified so that it contains many more exemplars of a target structure, in this case, the possessive determiners *his* and *her*. This text is taken from a collection of stories based on Chinese mythology. A sample from the original text is presented first followed by the flooded version. (Note: The items are bolded for the benefit of the reader of this text only. There is no need to include boldface when using input flood.)

(Original version)
Many moons ago there lived an officer in the Yellow Emperor's Imperial Guard named Hou Yi. Hou Yi was a skilled archer and **his** bow, no ordinary weapon, was enchanted. Hou Yi had married Chang E, the beautiful daughter of the River God. Hou Yi and Chang E were very much in love. They seemed happy, but, in fact, they wanted something more: Both Hou Yi and Chang E longed to live forever.

> —From "Moonbeams, Dumplings and Dragon Boats," Simonds & Swartz, 2002

(Flooded version)
Many moons ago there lived an officer in the Yellow Emperor's Imperial Guard named Hou Yi. Hou Yi was a skilled archer and *his* bow, no ordinary weapon, was enchanted. Hou Yi had married Chang E, the beautiful daughter of the River God. The day Hou Yi asked the River God for *his* daughter's hand in marriage, *her* father was deeply saddened because he knew he would miss seeing *her* charming face everyday. However, because Hou Yi was an excellent and loyal officer, the River God decided to grant *his* wish and gave him *his* daughter. He looked at Chang E lovingly, took *her* hand and gave her to *her* new husband. Hou Yi and Chang E were very much in love. They seemed very happy, but, in fact, they wanted something more: Hou Yi and *his* wife, Chang E, longed to live forever.

Notice how the input in the original text was modified so that it contains many more exemplars of possessive determiners. The original text contained 33 exemplars of possessive determiners. In the flooded version, there were 65. The essential meaning of the story, however, did not change. A piece of input was simply saturated so that learners could encounter many more instances of the target item.

The above example serves to illustrate how input flood can be carried out with an authentic text. Instructors, of course, could also choose to create their own texts to carry out input flood as with the following French example. The target structures here are the prepositions *à* and *en* used with geographical locations (both mean "to" or "in" depending on context). In French, the preposition *à* is used with cities and *en* with countries of feminine grammatical gender. Since this is an instructor generated text, there is only the flooded version (Again, the bolding of the targets is for the benefit of the reader of this text only).

> *Lise est célibataire et elle est le deuxième enfant des Pinard. Elle a 30 ans et elle est professeur de français **en** Angleterre. Lise aime beaucoup les langues et voyager. Lise parle français, italien, allemand et anglais. Actuellement, Lise habite **à** Londres, mais l'an prochain, elle va aller **en** Chine dans le cadre d'un programme d'échange. Elle va enseigner le français dans une université **à** Shanghai et en même temps, elle apprendra le chinois.*

> Lise is single and she is the second child of the Pinard family. She is 20 years old and she is a French teacher **in** England. Lise likes languages and traveling very much. Lise speaks French, Italian, German and English. Currently, Lise lives **in** London, but next year, she will go **to** China as part of an exchange program. She will teach French in a university **in** Shanghai and at the same time, she will learn Chinese.

In the complete version of this teacher generated text, out of 335 words there were 14 instances of the target structure. The number of exemplars, however, is not the issue here. There is currently no recipe to dictate how many exemplars is optimal for an input flood. However, if frequency may impact noticing as Gass (1997) suggests, then we may perhaps conclude that the more exemplars we can work in a flood the better. Furthermore, I should point out that it is not necessary to provide all the exemplars in the same text or even present all the exemplars or texts on the same day. In one use of input flood (Overstreet, 2000), multiple texts were provided over 2 weeks. In that particular instance, learners were exposed to almost 100 examples of the target item. The key here is that there is a deliberate attempt to expose learners to many examples of the target item via meaning-bearing input.

One important factor that instructors do want to pay attention to in carrying out input flood is to make sure that the level of difficulty of the input is appropriate for the learners in question. Recall that good input needs to be comprehensible. If learners need to struggle with extracting meaning from the text, they will probably not notice the flooded target structures no matter how frequently they may appear in the input.

Does Input Flood Work?

A handful of studies have investigated what learners can be expected to do after exposure to input that has been flooded with target forms. We will review two sample studies here.

One of the first empirical studies on input flood was conducted by Trahey and White (1993). These researchers wanted to know whether input flood would be effective in teaching young French-speaking ESL learners (ages 10–12) adverb placement in English. Adverb placement is a challenge for these learners because the rules for adverb placement in French are different from English. For example, English allows the following sentences:

> John watches TV often.
>
> John often watches TV.

but English does not allow the adverb to come between the verb and the object that follows it (an asterisk means a sentence is not grammatically correct):

> *John watches often TV.

French is similar to English in one adverb construction:

> *Jean regard la télé souvent.*
>
> John watches TV often.

but different from English in that it allows the following that include an adverb between the verb and object:

> *Jean regard souvent la télé.*
>
> *John watches often TV.

and does not allow the adverb to precede the verb as English does:

> *Jean souvent regard la télé.*
>
> John often watches TV.

Trahey and White saturated the input that these young learners received with hundreds of instances of English adverbs over a two-week period. Keep in mind that they were never explicitly taught the rules for adverb placement nor were they ever given any error correction. Adverbs were simply embedded in their instructional materials (i.e., stories and games). Overall, the results of this study showed that the input flood was effective in helping the students learn which adverb placement positions were possible in English. However, the flood did not appear to be effective in helping them learn which positions were *not* possible. For example, the flood enabled them to learn that in English, it is possible to have an adverb between the subject and the verb as in the sentence *Anna carefully drives her new car* (this is not permissible in French but permissible in English as we saw above). However, they also thought that sentences such as **Anna drives carefully her new car* (permissible in French but not in English) were also correct. Thus, the results of this study suggest that input flood may help provide learners with information about what is correct or what might be lacking in their linguistic system but it may not be very effective in showing them what is *not* correct.

Pause to consider . . .

Trahey and White's study. In this study, learners learned what was possible but not what was prohibited. What does this suggest about input flood as a technique? Do you think the results would have been different if they had picked a structure like third-person *-s* (e.g., he talks)? How is this structure different from adverb placement?

Another study on input flood was conducted by Williams and Evans (1998). These researchers wanted to see how input flood and a second condition in which learners were also given explicit rules and feedback could impact the learning of two target forms: participial adjectives (e.g., a *closed* door) and the passive construction in English (e.g., The door *was closed* by 9:00.). The subjects for this study were adult ESL learners. In the input flood condition, the learners received a flood of input that contained the target forms via a series of reading materials. No explicit rules or instructions were provided, and no corrective feedback was given. The second condition in this experiment was called the "instruction condition." The researchers called this the instruction condition because in addition to the flooded input, these learners were also taught the rules underlying the use of the target forms and were given feedback during activities. Overall, the results showed that for the participial adjective form, both the input flood group and the instructed group made improvements on posttests that tested this form. However, the group that received rules and feedback in addition to input flood had higher scores. For the passive construction, both the input flood group and the instructed group again made significant improvements from pretest to posttest but this time, there was not a significant difference between these two groups. In other words, both groups performed just as well. What these results suggest is that the target form can make a difference. Having rules and feedback in addition to input flood was more effective than input flood alone when the target form was participial adjectives (as measured by the posttests). However, when the form was the passive construction, having rules and feedback did not matter. Input flood by itself was just as effective.

Pause to consider . . .

the roles of explicit rules and feedback. In the Williams and Evans study, giving learners rules and feedback helped for one target form but not for another. What do these results suggest about the role of explicit rules and feedback in L2 instruction in general? Do you think that explicit instruction is necessary or beneficial no matter what technique or what form?

What observations could we make about the effectiveness of input flood from these two experiments? Before drawing any conclusions, we should first consider the contexts in which the two experiments were conducted. The subjects in Trahey and White's study were children between the ages of 10–12. They were native speakers of French learning English as a foreign language. The participants in Williams and Evans' study were adults learning English as a second language. The target structures under investigation as well as the research questions asked in the two studies were also different so we need to be cautious when comparing the two studies. With these cautions and limitations in mind, we may glean a few insights about input flood from these studies. One observation is that input flood did cause some learning to happen in both studies. In the Trahey and White study, input flood helped the learners realize that in English, adverbs can be placed in some positions that are not possible in French. In the Williams and Evans study, learners performed better on tests that measured participial adjectives and the passive construction after they received input that was flooded with the target structures. This suggests that exposing learners to meaning-bearing input that has been saturated with the target form can have a positive impact on SLA (at least in these two research contexts). Some limitations, however, also can be observed. Input flood does not appear to be effective in showing learners what is not possible in the target language (at least for learning adverb placement). Recall that in the Trahey and White study, the learners continued to think that the incorrect adverb positions were possible in English. Here is a case, perhaps, where learners might benefit from explicit information. Because learners cannot know from input alone what is not possible in an L2, being explicitly told so might help them process input more efficiently. Nevertheless, the finding that input flood alone can lead to some kind of learning shows that this technique can have some kind of impact on SLA.

Pause to consider . . .

the difference between the Trahey and White (1993) and Williams and Evans (1998) studies. One of the differences between the two studies was the age of the participants. How might you design an experiment to investigate whether the age of learners is an important factor when examining the effectiveness of input flood?

What Are the Advantages and Disadvantages of Input Flood in the L2 Classroom?

One of the main advantages of input flood is that it involves the provision of lots of meaning-bearing input. As we saw in Chapter 3, meaning-bearing input is an essential ingredient of SLA. Another advantage of this technique is that it does not disrupt the flow of communication or the focus of any communicative activity. Doughty and Williams (1998) describe input flood as one of the least *obtrusive* techniques because the learners' attention can remain focused on the meaningful task at hand (p. 258). When we say that a technique is not obtrusive, we mean that the teacher does not stop an activity or exchange to point anything out. Input flood, then, is ideal for meaning-based approaches where the primary focus of the class is always on meaning and meaningful interaction. Content and task-based L2 classes are examples of such meaning-based classes. As you may recall from Chapter 1, in a content class, learners learn different subject matters such as geography, history and economics in the L2. In a task-based class, the goal of each lesson is to complete specific tasks. Input flood could easily be worked into the course materials of such classes. For example, in a history class on the French Revolution, the instructor could simply manipulate lecture notes and reading materials so that this input contains many uses of a particular target form. That's all the instructor would need to do. In fact, another advantage of this technique is that it is easy to use. No special teaching or explaining is needed. All the instructor needs to do is saturate the input with the target form.

Of course, a disadvantage of input flood is that because this technique is so *implicit*, it is difficult for instructors to know whether learners are actually learning anything through the flood. By implicit, I mean that other than embedding the form in the input, nothing else is done to point out the form to the learner. Thus, we cannot be sure that learners will actually notice the form. Sharwood Smith further reminds us that we can only expect input enhancement to increase the chance that learners will notice the form. There is no guarantee that they actually will. What input flood does guarantee is a good dose of meaning-bearing input that can be injected virtually anywhere in a lesson plan.

Pause to consider . . .

the nature of foreign language classes in the United States. Many classes are built around a structural syllabus. Such a syllabus is structured around grammatical features, for example, the first chapter may be on the present tense or particular aspects of the present tense. Can we use input flood with such a syllabus where there may be a new grammar topic presented each day? If you used input flood to teach grammar, how might you test grammar?

How Do We Implement Input Flood in the L2 Classroom?

We mentioned earlier that input flood is ideal for meaning-based classrooms but this technique can actually be adapted for use in virtually any type of classroom. If there is a structure that learners need to pay more attention to, instructors could simply modify some of the material to include a flood of that structure for a period of time. Target items could be embedded in existing instructional materials such as readings, games, and other activities and exercises. Instructors could even flood their instructions to students or other classroom-management agenda items with the target items. Here is an example of how an instructor might give instructions with input flood. The target form here is the 2nd person plural subjunctive form in French (the forms are underlined for the benefit of the reader only).

> *Il faut que vous <u>arriviez</u> en classe à l'heure demain. Nous avons un examen. Il est pertinent que vous <u>étudiez</u> bien ce soir. Il est nécessaire que vous <u>révisiez</u> les chapitres trois, quatre et cinq ainsi que les lectures supplémentaires. N'oubliez pas votre cahier d'exercises. Il est préférable que vous <u>complétiez</u> les exercises avant d'aller en classe. Comme je vous ai dit la dernière fois, il est nécessaire que vous <u>corrigiez</u> tous les exercises avant de me les rendre. N'oubliez pas vos crayons. Il est préférable que vous <u>écriviez</u> vos examens en crayon. Avez-vous des questions?*

It is necessary that you <u>arrive</u> to class on time tomorrow. We have a test. It's pertinent that you <u>study</u> well this evening. It's necessary that you <u>review</u> chapters three, four and five as well as the supplementary readings. Don't forget your workbook. It's preferred that you <u>complete</u> the exercises before going to class. As I told you last time, it's necessary that you <u>correct</u> all the exercises before you turn them into me. Don't forget your pencils. It's preferred that you <u>write</u> your exams in pencil. Any questions?

Additionally, in actual language classrooms, instructors do not have to be limited to one type of input enhancement. Instructors can and often should make use of many techniques at the same time to meet their needs. We said earlier that because input flood is so implicit, we may not know whether learners actually do notice the forms in the flood. To increase the likelihood that they will notice them, the instructor could explicitly tell learners to pay attention to the forms or they could have learners perform a task with the flooded input that would require them to notice the target forms. For example, in the flooded text presented earlier based on Chinese mythology, learners may be asked to answer comprehension questions that require them to notice and process possessive determiners correctly in order to arrive at the correct responses.

The following story is a tale from Chinese mythology. Read each section of the story carefully and answer the questions that follow. We will go over the answers together after each section.

The Story of Hou Yi and Chang E

Many moons ago there lived an officer in the Yellow Emperor's Imperial Guard named Hou Yi. Hou Yi was a skilled archer and his bow, no ordinary weapon, was enchanted. Hou Yi had married Chang E, the beautiful daughter of the River God. The day Hou Yi asked the River God for his daughter's hand in marriage, her father was deeply saddened because he knew he would miss seeing her charming face everyday. However, because Hou Yi was an excellent and loyal officer, the River God decided to grant his wish and gave him his daughter. He looked at Chang E lovingly, took her hand and gave her to her new husband. Hou Yi and Chang E were very much in love. They seemed very happy, but, in fact, they wanted something more: Both Hou Yi and Chang E longed to live forever.

1. Who is Hou Yi?
   a. The River God
   b. An officer
2. Whose face would the River God miss seeing?
   a. Chang E's face.
   b. Hou Yi's face.
3. Whose wish did the River God grant?
   a. Chang E's wish.
   b. Hou Yi's wish.
4. Whose hand did the River God take?
   a. Hou Yi's hand.
   b. Chang E's hand.
5. What did Hou Yi and Chang E wish for?
   a. To forever stay in love.
   b. To have immortality.

As this example illustrates, the second, third, and fourth comprehension questions encourage learners to notice the target forms, that is to say, possessive determiners *his* and *her*. For example, in order to answer the second question correctly, learners have to pay attention to the possessive determiner *her* in the phrase "... *he would miss seeing her charming face everyday*," and understand that *her* refers to Chang E (it is assumed that learners know that Chang E is a woman's name and that Hou Yi is a man's name). As you can see, this type of activity would encourage learners to pay attention to the flooded forms in the input.

Bardovi-Harlig and Reynolds (1995) propose that learners be directed to perform *focused-noticing exercises* with the flooded input. In order to encourage learners to notice the difference between their own grammars and the target grammar, they propose that learners be explicitly directed to notice the use of the target form-meaning associations through exercises such as the following on past tense verbs (p. 123):

a. [based on the reading passage], find a sentence with one verb in the simple past. Write it on the line below.
b. Find a sentence with one simple past verb and one past progressive verb. Write it on the line below.
c. Kerwin [the narrator] used the following verbs in the past progressive. He also used them in the simple past. Find the simple past forms, write them beside the past progressive and write the line where you found them. Look at the way the past progressive and the simple past are used. Can you tell a difference in meaning?

Past Progressive (lines 1–2)	Simple Past	Line
was walking (lines 1–2)	_____	_____
was doing (lines 55–56)	_____	_____

The point here is that instructors do not need to rely on input flood alone to draw learners' attention to form if such a technique is adopted. Instructors could lead learners to perform focusing activities based on the flood or they could use the flood in conjunction with other techniques. The main benefit of a flood is that learners are given a shot of extra meaning-bearing input, input that is fundamental for acquisition. If instructors wish to make the forms in that input more salient, more explicit techniques could be added (as discussed in later chapters in this book).

Remember to Keep Meaning in Focus

In attempting to flood classroom input with exemplars of the target, instructors must not lose sight of the primary goal of language: to communicate meaning. While it may be desirable to expose learners to lots of examples of the target, this must not be done at the expense of meaning and authentic communication. This is important to point out because it is sometimes easy to get carried away with trying to find opportunities to embed the target form. When this happens, meaning may be compromised and language may become unnatural. In such cases, language may no longer be used for communication but for display purposes only. When using input flood, instructors should ask: "Once learners listen to or read the input, what are they supposed to do?" In order for the flood to be meaningful, they must do something with the input. If you look at the sample activities in this chapter and the Appendix, you will notice that learners don't just read or listen. They are required to *respond to the input* in some way. In short, we don't just "throw" the input at them. In the above example where we flooded the instructions with the target form (i.e., the French subjunctive), learners were expected to follow the instructors' instructions after listening to them. Here are some examples of other things learners could be expected to do after receiving flooded input:

- take a quiz on the content;
- answer questions based on the flooded input;
- perform some kind of task based on the flooded input (e.g., reconstruct a story, draw a picture based on oral directions, play a game, etc.)

The point here is that input flood does not stop with simply giving learners the input; learners must do something meaningful with that flooded input.

Pause to consider . . .

this idea of having to do something with the input you are exposed to. Look once again at this chapter's example in French in which the teacher gives instructions and embeds multiple examples of the second-person plural of the subjunctive. How could the teacher follow these instructions with a task for the learners that shows if they were paying attention? Note: the answer is *not* to provide a quiz on the forms in question!

SUMMARY/CONCLUSION

As this chapter has demonstrated, input flood has many potential uses for the classroom. Input flood is a good way to provide learners with the meaning-bearing input that they need for SLA while exposing them to lots of examples of particular L2 items at the same time. Research has shown that when learners receive enough of this input, they may notice these features more. Another advantage of input flood is that it is very versatile. Input flood can be integrated with virtually any teaching approach, lesson plan, activity or exercise. In the next chapter, we will see how input flood can be integrated with what is called "textual enhancement."

ENHANCE YOUR KNOWLEDGE

Input Enhancement Techniques

Doughty, J., & Williams, J. (1998). Pedagogical choices in focus on form. In C. Doughty & J. Williams (Eds.), *Focus on form in second language classroom acquisition* (pp. 197–261). Cambridge, MA: Cambridge University Press.

Input Flood

Trahey, M. & White, L. (1993). Positive evidence and preemption in the second language classroom. *Studies in Second Language Acquisition, 15*, 181–204.
White, J. (1998). Getting the learners' attention: A typographical input enhancement study. In C. Doughty & J. Williams (Eds.), *Focus on form in second language classroom acquisition* (pp. 91–128). Cambridge, MA: Cambridge University Press.
Williams, J., & Evans, J. (1998). What kind of focus and on which forms? In C. Doughty & J. Williams (Eds.), *Focus on form in second language classroom acquisition* (pp. 139–155). Cambridge, MA: Cambridge University Press.

CHAPTER 5

Textual Enhancement

WHAT IS TEXTUAL ENHANCEMENT?

Have you ever seen a text like the following?

Unitarianism: A Foundation for Liberal Theology

Unitarians and liberals agree on certain key points:
They do not believe that the Bible is the Word of God. Some of them say parts of it may contain the Word of God mixed in with superstition.

They not only deny that the Bible is the Word of God, but also **deny the Christian doctrines that are derived from it.**

They do not think that God is a person. They think of Him as a Force, an Oversoul, a Prime Mover, or even as being dead!

They think of Jesus as merely a man, an exceptional man like Moses and Buddha, but not more than a man. In their view Jesus' main contribution was as a teacher.
—From "So What's the Difference," Ridenour, 1967

Did you notice the bolding and italics in the text? What do you think is the function of using these typographical cues? If you said "to remember a main concept" you are correct. Using typographical cues such as bolding and italics to draw the reader's attention to particular information in a text is known as **textual enhancement.** What you saw in the above text is an example of textual enhancement used in a first-language context. The author bolded and italicized information in the text that he wanted his readers to pay special attention to.

Textual enhancement is also used in the context of SLA but its purpose is different. In an L2 context, textual enhancement is used to draw language learners' attention to grammatical form. If, for example, learners forget to put an -s at the end of third-person singular verbs, the instructor could typographically enhance the -s on all third-person singular verbs in their reading materials.

This is essentially the idea behind textual enhancement: to render more salient particular features of written input that learners normally may not notice and make form-meaning connections for. For example, a learner may not notice a particular form because the form is not very important to the meaning of the message. Or perhaps the form is not perceptually salient, that is to say, the form is easy for the eye to miss. Textual enhancement could be used in these cases to make these forms more salient. The desired outcome is that learners will notice these enhanced forms and then make form-meaning connections from them.

Pause to consider . . .

the saliency of different forms. What are some forms in the target language you teach that are not salient? What factors do you think could affect the salience of a form?

How Is Textual Enhancement Carried Out?

Like with all the techniques presented in this book, textual enhancement begins with meaning-bearing input. In this case, the input is written. This could be in the form of a letter, an article, a story or anything else that is written meaning-bearing input. The target item in this input is then *enhanced* by visually altering its appearance in the text. For example, the target item could be *italicized,* **bolded,** or <u>underlined</u>. The font and character size or style could be altered or highlighting with color could be applied. If desired, different types of typographical manipulation could also be used at the same time.

Pause to consider . . .

textual enhancement with oral input. How could you enhance oral input? Do you think it makes sense to enhance oral input? Or does it not make sense to alter input this way?

If your sample of written input does not contain many exemplars of the target form, then you may find it necessary to modify the text so that you could add more exemplars to it. In this way, the procedure involved in textual enhancement is similar to the procedure for preparing written input flood. Additional exemplars of your target form need to be embedded if the original text does not contain many examples of the form. The difference is that in textual enhancement, the target form is also typographically altered to enhance its perceptual salience. The following is an example of what an unenhanced and an enhanced text may look like. The text is taken from the French tale *Le petit prince* by Antoine de Saint Exupéry. The target forms are the indefinite articles *un* and *une* in French. In French, articles must agree with the gender of the noun it modifies: *un* for masculine nouns and *une* for feminine nouns.

(Unenhanced Version)
Lorsque j'avais six ans, j'ai vu une fois une magnifique image, dans un livre sur la fôret vierge qui s'appelait «Histoires vécues». Ça représentait un serpent boa qui avalait un fauve. Voilà une copie du dessin.

(Once when I was six years old, I saw a wonderful picture in a book on the virgin forest entitled "Stories Lived." This picture showed a boa snake who was swallowing a wildcat. Here is a copy of the drawing.)

(Enhanced Version)
Lorsque j'avais six ans, j'ai vu **une** fois **une** magnifique image, dans **un** livre sur la fôret vierge qui s'appelait «Histoires vécues». Ça représentait **un** serpent boa qui avalait **un** fauve. Voilà **une** copie du dessin.

Do you see how the forms stand out so much more in the second bolded version? A different cue could also be assigned to the feminine article to bring out the difference between masculine and feminine forms such as in the following example:

Lorsque j'avais six ans, j'ai vu _*une*_ fois _*une*_ magnifique image, dans _*un*_ livre sur la fôret vierge qui s'appelait «Histoires vécues». Ça représentait _*un*_ serpent boa qui avalait _*un*_ fauve. Voilà _*une*_ copie du dessin.

In the above version, all the targets are italicized, underlined and in a larger character size. As you can see, the *-e* of the feminine article is also bolded in order to bring out the difference between the feminine and masculine articles.

I should point out that all the input flood materials that we saw in Chapter 4 could also be used as textual enhancement materials. We would just need to typographically enhance all the target forms.

The next text is an example of how verbal morphology could be enhanced. The passage, a Spanish version of *Little Red Riding Hood* from Jourdenais, Ota, Stauffer, Boyson and Doughty (1998), was used in a study by Overstreet (1998). (Note: The original authors did not enhance them this way nor did Overstreet.) The target form is the preterit tense. For each target, the entire verb is underlined and the morphological ending is bolded to draw learners' attention to it.

Cuando Caperucita <u>lle**gó**</u>, el lobo <u>imi**tó**</u> la voz de la abuela. Caperucita <u>pregun**tó**</u> al lobo por qué tenía esos ojos y esas orejas tan grandes. El lobo <u>respon**dió**</u> que para verla y oirla mejor. En seguida, Caperucita <u>pregun**tó**</u> por qué tenía la boca tan grande.

(When Little Red Riding Hood arrived, the wolf imitated Grandmother's voice. Little Red Riding Hood asked the wolf why he had such big eyes and ears. The wolf answered that it was to see and hear her better. Then, Little Red Riding Hood asked why he had such a big mouth.)

As these examples illustrate, there are many ways to enhance a text. Whether there are better ways than others to carry out the enhancement is a question that researchers are still investigating.

Pause to consider . . .

the various ways you could typographically enhance a form. You have seen three different ways that typographical cues may be used to enhance a form. What are some other ways? Do you think there are better ways than others to enhance? What do you think is the best way?

Does Textual Enhancement Work?

Quite a few studies have been conducted to evaluate whether textual enhancement is effective in getting language learners to pay attention to target forms. I will discuss a handful of these studies in detail here. A list of textual enhancement studies is included at the end of this chapter.

One of the first studies to examine textual enhancement in an L2 context was Shook (1994). In addition to investigating whether textual enhancement was effective, Shook also wanted to see if explicitly telling learners to pay attention to the enhanced forms might make a difference. Shook used two target forms in his study: the present perfect and the relative pronouns *que* and *quien* in Spanish. The subjects for his study were Spanish learners from first- and second-year college Spanish courses. Three groups were used in this study. In the first group, the subjects read enhanced versions of the texts and were also told to pay attention to the enhanced target items. The second group also read enhanced versions of the texts but they were not told to pay attention to the enhanced items. The third group, the control group, read the same texts but these texts were not typographically enhanced and these subjects were not told to pay attention to anything in particular. The target forms in the enhanced versions of the texts were enhanced by using a larger character size, retyping the forms in upper case letters and by bolding them. A series of assessment tasks were used to measure the subjects' ability to recognize the target forms as well as to produce them. Overall, the results revealed that the two groups that read the enhanced texts performed significantly better than the control group that read the unenhanced texts on all the assessment tasks. This shows that the enhancement did make a difference. Reading the enhanced texts allowed the subjects to recognize and produce the forms better. There was no difference between those subjects who had explicit instruction to pay attention to the enhancement and those who did not get these explicit instructions.

This means that the explicit direction to pay attention did not matter. Reading the enhanced texts was enough to allow the subjects to make improvements on the assessment tasks. The type of target form, however, appeared to affect the results. Shook found that overall, scores on the present perfect tests were higher than scores on the relative pronoun tests. Shook thinks that subjects performed better on the present perfect forms because this form has a higher communicative value than relative pronouns. **Communicative value** refers to the overall importance the form plays in determining the meaning of a piece of input. When Shook said that the present perfect tense has a higher communicative value he meant that this form was more important than the relative pronoun forms to understanding the meaning of the texts. If learners skipped over relative pronouns, this would not affect the meaning of the texts very much but the same cannot be said for the present perfect tense forms. If they missed present perfect forms, they might have missed the temporal reference of the text which would interfere with their comprehension of the text. Thus, Shook believed that his subjects paid more attention to the enhanced present perfect forms because these forms were more important for understanding the overall meaning of the text.

Another study conducted on textual enhancement was Alanen (1995). In this study, Alanen wanted to see if giving learners explicit rules about the target form would make a difference. The targets of instruction were grammatical morphemes in an artificial language based on Finnish (Alanen called them semi-artificial locative suffixes and consonant gradation in Finnish). The subjects for this study were adult native speakers of English. In Group One, the subjects were first given rules explaining the use of the target forms and then they were given texts to read in which the target forms were italicized. In Group Two, subjects were given the rules only. They did not get any texts to read. In Group Three, the subjects were given the enhanced texts only. They did not receive the explicit information that Group One and Group Two got. Group Four read unenhanced versions of the text only and they were not given any rules about the forms.

As the subjects read their texts, they were all asked to think aloud and their verbalizations were tape-recorded. The think-aloud data showed that the subjects who read the texts with the target forms italicized (i.e., Group One and Group Three) made more mention of the target forms than those who read the unenhanced versions (Group Four) and those who did not have texts to read (Group Two). This shows that the enhancement was effective in helping the subjects notice the targets. However, the results of a production task revealed that while all the subjects who read the enhanced texts (Group One and Group Three) learned more than those in who read the unenhanced versions (Group Four), those who got rules in addition to the enhanced texts did better (Group One). Additionally, those who got only rules (Group Two) did better than those who just got the enhanced texts (Group Three). What these findings tell us is that while textual enhancement was effective in helping learners notice the target forms (as seen in the think-aloud data), it was not as effective in helping the subjects use the forms. When learners had to use the forms correctly in production, giving them rules appeared to be better.

Pause to consider . . .

the explicit information groups in Alanen's study. In Alanen's study, the
experimental groups who got rules performed better on the assessment tasks
than those subjects who got enhanced texts alone without rules. Based on this
finding, should researchers conclude that learners will always need explicit
information in order to learn the target structures used in this study?

Overstreet (1998) wanted to see if giving learners familiar texts to read
would help them pay more attention to target forms. His idea was that if the
content of the texts were familiar, then learners would have an easier time with
comprehension and consequently might be able to pay more attention to the
enhanced forms. The subjects in Overstreet's study were third-semester university Spanish learners and the target forms were the preterit and imperfect tenses
in Spanish. One group of subjects read a text that contained familiar content
(*Little Red Riding Hood*) with the targets enhanced. A second group read a text
that contained unfamiliar content with the targets enhanced. A third group read
a text that contained the familiar content but the targets were unenhanced. A
fourth group read a text that contained the unfamiliar content with the targets
unenhanced. The imperfect tense forms were enhanced through underlining,
bolding and using a larger character size and a font that was different from the
rest of the text. The preterit forms were enhanced via underlining, shadowing
and using a larger character size and different font. Overstreet did not find that
textual enhancement helped the learners recognize or use the target forms correctly based on paper-and-pencil post-tests. Those who read the unenhanced
texts performed just as well as those who read the enhanced texts. The familiarity of the content also did not matter. Those who read the texts with unfamiliar
content performed the same as those who read the texts with the familiar
content. Overstreet was also interested in whether textual enhancement might
affect the learners' ability to comprehend the text so he gave all the subjects a
true-false comprehension test (in Spanish) on the content of the texts. Overstreet
found that textual enhancement did have an effect on comprehension. Those
who read the enhanced version of the texts had lower scores on comprehension
than those who read the unenhanced versions. This suggests that the enhancement might have interfered with learners' comprehension of the texts. Overstreet believes that by drawing learners' attention to the enhanced forms, the
subjects were not paying as much attention to meaning as they normally would
when there is no enhancement. This finding in Overstreet's study raises a potential concern regarding textual enhancement. Remember that acquisition is
intricately linked to comprehension. In order for form-meaning connections to
happen, learners must pay attention to both meaning and form. If comprehension does not happen, then there is a problem. It is also important to point out,
however, that Overstreet's study is the only study so far that has found a negative effect for textual enhancement on comprehension. Other textual enhancement studies that have examined its effects on comprehension have not found

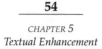
any effect (positive or negative) for this input enhancement technique on comprehension. Thus, it is possible that this negative effect in Overstreet's study could be due to other variables such as the assessment task he used to measure comprehension or perhaps even to the type of typograhical enhancement that he used. Nevertheless, Overstreet's finding is important to discuss because it speaks to the importance of meaning and comprehension in language instruction. When we try to get learners to pay attention to form through any kind of instructional technique, we must not lose sight of the importance of focusing on meaning.

Pause to consider . . .

the effect of textual enhancement on meaning. Although most studies do not show that textual enhancement negatively affects comprehension, one study (Overstreet, 1998) has. Do you think there is a potential for textual enhancement to have an affect on comprehension? Why? If it could have an effect, do you think this effect would always be negative or do you think the effect could also be positive?

A more recent study by Wong (2002b) investigated whether the level of input, that is to say, discourse level versus sentence level input, may have an impact on textual enhancement. In all the textual enhancement studies reviewed earlier, the input was discourse level input. Learners were given a text or texts to read in the form of a magazine or newspaper article or short story. Because it is generally easier for beginning learners of a new language to comprehend short sentences rather than a text, Wong hypothesized that providing textual enhancement via sentence level input might help learners notice the target features better. The target structure in Wong's study was prepositions used with geographical locations in French. In French, the preposition *à* is always used with cities to say that one is *in* a city—*à Paris, à Madrid* (in Paris, in Madrid)—and *en* is always used with countries that have a feminine gender—*en France, en Espagne* (in France, in Spain). The participants in this study were first-year university learners of French. One group of participants read a text (discourse-level input) with the target prepositions enhanced via bolding and italics. A second group of participants read the same text but the target forms were not typographically enhanced. A third group was given sentence-level input that contained visually enhanced target structures. A fourth group read the same set of sentences but these sentences were not visually enhanced. The text and input sentences were created by the researcher (see Appendix D for the text and input sentences). The results revealed that, overall, those who received textual enhancement performed better than those who did not get enhancement on a paper-and-pencil assessment task of the target structures. This means that the enhancement was successful in helping learners perform well on the assessment task regardless of whether the input was sentence level or discourse level. The results also showed that, overall, participants who received sentence level input performed better than those who received discourse level input, regardless of whether the input was enhanced or not. Thus, the general conclusions that may be drawn from this study are that textual enhancement was successful in helping learners perform well on the assessment task and that sentence level input was easier to process than discourse level input.

Pause to consider . . .

the text used in Wong's study. In earlier textual enhancement studies, the target structures were embedded in authentic texts such as magazine or newspaper articles. In Wong's study, the text that contained the target structures was a teacher-generated text. Do you think embedding target structures in a teacher-generated text versus an authentic text could have an impact on the results? How might you design an experiment to investigate this?

As the research findings reviewed above suggest, it is difficult to draw conclusions in regards to the effectiveness of textual enhancement as an input enhancement technique. It appears that textual enhancement is sometimes effective (e.g., Shook, Wong), sometimes it is only partly effective (e.g. Alanen) and at other times it is not very effective (e.g., Overstreet). What do you think is the reason for these mixed results? The answer may in part lie in the nature of the target items and the assessment tasks used to measure the effectiveness of textual enhancement. Shook found that textual enhancement was effective in helping his subjects recognize the target forms as well as to use them in production. However, he also found that the type of form also made a difference. Textual enhancement was more helpful for the present perfect forms than for the relative pronoun forms. Recall also that in Williams and Evans' study on input flood discussed in Chapter 4, these researchers also found that the type of target form made a difference in their results. It is possible then, that textual enhancement may be more helpful for certain forms than others. The type of assessment task used to measure the effectiveness of textual enhancement also seems to make a difference. In Alanen's study, the researcher included a think-aloud procedure and a production task. In the think-aloud task, the effectiveness of textual enhancement was based on how many times the subjects made a mention of the target forms as they read their texts. In the production task, the subjects were required to use the form correctly to make complete sentences. Additionally, they were asked to state the rules governing the use of the forms. As you can probably gather, simply mentioning that a target exists is very different from having to use the target correctly and knowing the rules governing the use of the target form. Based on the think-aloud data, it appears that textual enhancement is indeed effective in helping learners notice the forms because all the subjects who read the enhanced texts in Alanen's study mentioned more target forms than those who read the unenhanced versions. Other textual enhancement studies that have think-aloud data also confirm this finding (e.g., Jourdenais, Ota, Stauffer, Boyson and Doughty, 1995). However, when learners are also required to produce or recognize the correct use of the form, the results are less conclusive. For some forms, textual enhancement can also help learners recognize and use the form (e.g., Shook and Wong). For other forms, it is not effective (e.g., Overstreet) or less effective than giving learners explicit rules about the form (e.g., Alanen). The level of input also appears to make a difference. Wong's study lends support to the idea that when comprehension is less demanding, such as in sentence level input, learners may be more likely to direct their attention to grammatical form. More research of this nature is needed to further explore this possibility.

Pause to consider . . .

the mixed research findings. We just talked about how the nature of the target form and the type of assessment task used in textual enhancement studies can impact research results. What are some other possible factors?

WHAT ARE THE ADVANTAGES AND DISADVANTAGES OF TEXTUAL ENHANCEMENT IN THE L2 CLASSROOM?

One of the advantages of textual enhancement is that it draws on the provision of meaning-bearing input, a very necessary ingredient of SLA. Textual enhancement directs learners' attention to form while also encouraging them to process meaning-bearing input for meaning. Another advantage is that textual enhancement can be easily integrated into different types of instruction. Like with written input flood, textual enhancement could easily be worked into various course materials regardless of the teaching approach advocated. If course readings contain exemplars of the target form, instructors could simply enhance those forms by manipulating the typographical cues so learners' attention will be drawn to these items. As with input flood, textual enhancement is easy to use and is unobtrusive to communication and to the task at hand.

A disadvantage of textual enhancement is that we do not always know what learners are learning from the enhanced input. We saw from the research findings in the previous section that textual enhancement may be effective in helping learners notice the forms that we enhance but we cannot be sure whether they actually make form-meaning connections from that enhanced input. In the studies reviewed, when learners were asked to either recognize the form in subsequent input or asked to use the form correctly in production, sometimes they could and sometimes they could not. It appears that when understanding the function of the form is crucial, this technique is not always effective. Another disadvantage of textual enhancement is that there is a potential for this technique to detract learners' attention from meaning. As shown in Overstreet's study, when we draw learners' attention to form, there is a possibility that they will pay less attention to meaning. Thus, when we use this technique, we need to make sure that learners are also pushed to attend to meaning.

> ## Pause to consider . . .
>
> noticing versus understanding a form. We just saw that textual enhancement is effective in helping learners notice target forms but it is not always effective in getting them to understand the function of the form or use it in production. Do you think it is necessary that learners always understand and be able to use the form the first time they notice it?

HOW DO WE IMPLEMENT TEXTUAL ENHANCEMENT IN THE L2 CLASSROOM?

Implementing textual enhancement in the classroom is very easy. If you are a language instructor, you probably already make use of typographical cues to draw your students' attention to important information when you write on the board or create homework assignments for them. If there is a particular grammatical form that you think your students need to pay more attention to, you could simply enhance that form each time it appears in the written materials you use for your class. For example, if you teach English and you notice that your students have trouble with regular simple past tense forms (e.g., talk**ed**), you could simply enhance all these forms in their reading materials. If the target form does not appear frequently in the materials, then the input in the readings could also be manipulated so that more exemplars of the enhanced forms may be embedded. Additionally, new texts could also be created to simultaneously address the course content at hand and draw learners' attention to forms that they may need to pay more attention to. Furthermore, unlike a research experiment where variables need to be isolated and highly controlled, instructors in actual classrooms may make use of different input enhancement techniques when they teach. Thus, there is no reason why textual enhancement cannot be used in conjunction with other input enhancement techniques. An instructor may choose to rely on more explicit techniques such as structured input activities (see Chapter 6) to encourage both noticing and a deeper processing of the target forms and then use textual enhancement to reinforce what was learned by giving learners texts to read with the target forms enhanced. Or, textual enhancement may be used as a priming activity to first get learners to notice the forms. Instructors could then follow up with activities that will push them to process those forms more deeply. The following are some general guidelines to consider if instructors should want to implement textual enhancement in their lesson plans.

Determine the Goal of Instruction

What role is textual enhancement expected to play in a given lesson? Is the goal merely to use textual enhancement to help learners notice the targets or is more extensive processing desired? Will textual enhancement be the only type of input enhancement used to reach the instructional goal or will other techniques also be employed?

Choose an Appropriate Form

We saw in the previous sections that the type of form we enhance may have an impact on the effectiveness of textual enhancement. Textual enhancement may be more effective for some forms than others. Imagine that you are a beginning learner of English and you come across the following passages:

1. My cousin Billy and I have a lot of <u>pets</u>. I have two <u>cats</u>. Billy has only one <u>cat</u>. I have only one <u>hamster</u> but Billy has four <u>hamsters</u>. Billy has a <u>bird</u> named Polly. I have two <u>birds</u>. Their names are Tweety and Chirpy. My older sister has a <u>dog</u>. Someday I would like to have three <u>dogs</u>.

2. I **must** get more sleep. If not, I **may** not wake up for work. I **may** have to drink lots of coffee and then I **may** be nervous all day. It **must** be close to midnight right now. I **must** stop staying up so late at night.

You probably noticed the enhancement in both passages but which passage might help you make better form-meaning connections from the enhanced input? If you said the first one you are right. The first passage is easier because the target forms have a **transparent form-function** (or **form-meaning**) **relationship.** This means that the form has a relatively distinct meaning or function that corresponds to it. The form plural -*s* in English has a distinct corresponding meaning: it expresses plurality (*cat* vs. *cats*). When we enhance forms that have a clear form-meaning or form-function relationship, the enhancement will draw learners' attention to these forms and as a result, they may see this relationship better. The second passage is more difficult because the modal auxiliaries *may* and *must* do not have a clear form-function or form-meaning relationship. The modal auxiliary *may* expresses possibility (*I **may** go to the back today*) but it can also express the idea of giving permission (***May** I get a drink of water?*). The modal auxiliary *must* expresses necessity (*I **must** study more.*) but it can also express probability (*That **must** be our professor over there*). Thus, even though the enhancement in this text made the target forms more salient, learners may still have a hard time seeing their form-meaning relationship.

In French, the function of the prepositions *à* and *en* to express "in" with geographical locations could also be said to be transparent. The preposition *à* is always used with cities—*à Paris, à Madrid* (in Paris, in Madrid)—and *en* is always used with countries that have a feminine gender—*en France, en Espagne* (in France, in Spain). This may also in part explain why Wong's study found favorable results for textual enhancement whereas other studies did not.

In Spanish, an example of a form that does not have a clear form-meaning relationship is the choice of the copular verbs *ser* and *estar*. Although both verbs can be mutually exclusive in a variety of contexts, they can both also co-occur with a variety of (thought not all) adjectives. The distinction in meaning has to do with what linguists call perfectivity. "Perfectivity" is used to refer to states or events that imply a beginning or end, especially from a speaker's perspective. We tend to use *ser* to express ideas that do not have a definitive beginning and end (e.g., The sun is shining) and *estar* to express idea that do (e.g., John is making dinner). However, there are contexts where the distinction is not always clear. Take the adjective, *young*, for example. Would you use *ser* or *estar* with the adjective? If you're 25, you may think that a 69-year-old is an old person. However, to an 80-year-old, a 69-year-old is still young. Thus, the choice of *estar* and *ser* here would depend on the perspective of the person making the statement. Can you see how the relationship between these verbs and their meanings is not so obvious? When we enhance such forms, learners may have more difficulty connecting the form to its meaning or function no matter how salient the enhancement may be.

Pause to consider . . .

forms that do not have a clear corresponding meaning or function. Should we bother to enhance these forms?

Choose a Text That Is Appropriate to the Level of Your Students

Remember that when your students read a text, they are supposed to read the text for comprehension. If your text is difficult, your learners will need to devote most of their attention to understanding the meaning of the text and as a result, they may not pay attention to the enhanced forms. As Wong's study using sentence level input suggests, the easier comprehension is, the more likely your learners will be able to notice the enhanced forms and make form-meaning connections from them.

Consider the Frequency of Exposure

You also need to think about how much exposure you want your learners to have to the enhanced forms. This will of course depend on the role that textual enhancement is expected to play and the time that is available for instruction. Keep in mind that learners may be exposed to one text with many exemplars or several texts with more or less exemplars. You could also give learners multiple exposures over an extended period of time.

Pause to consider . . .

how you want to expose your learners to the enhancement. Do you think it's better to give learners one text to read that contains many examples of the form or several texts that contain fewer instances of the form? Why?

Consider How You Will Use the Typographical Cues

There are many different ways to enhance the forms in your text and the type of cues you use could have an impact on the effectiveness of the enhancement. A study by Simard (2001) found that different cues and different combination of cues could lead to different results. Thus, you need to think about which cues will help you best obtain the results you want. Will you enhance the entire word or only part of the word? Will you use italics, caps, or bolding? Will you just use one cue or will you use a combination of different cues?

In the studies on enhanced verbal morphology, some have enhanced entire verbs (e.g., Overstreet, 1998) while others either enhanced only the inflectional ending or used a different type of cue to enhance the ending (e.g., Leow, 2001). The following is an example from Jourdenais, Ota, Stauffer, Boyson and Doughty (1995) that Overstreet used in his study (1998). Notice how entire verbs are enhanced here. All the targets were enlarged and underlined. Additionally, he used one type of font for the imperfect and another for the present perfect.

> <u>Había</u> una vez una chica que <u>vivía</u> en el bosque. Caperucita roja, ese <u>era</u> su nombre porque siempre <u>llevaba</u> una capa roja, <u>visitaba</u> a su abuela los fines de semana. Un día, la madre le <u>dijo</u>: "Caperucita, anda visita a la abuela, que está enferma, y llévale esta canasta de comida."

> (Once upon a time there was a girl who lived in the woods. Little Red Riding Hood, this was her name because she always wore a red hood, visited her grandmother on the weekends. One day, her mother said to her: "Little Red Riding Hood, go visit Grandmother, who is sick, and bring her this basket of food.")

Here is an alternate way of enhancing the same text.

> *Había* una vez una chica que *vivía* en el bosque. Caperucita roja, ese *era* su nombre porque siempre *llevaba* una capa roja, *visitaba* a su abuela los fines de semana. Un día, la madre le *dijo*: "Caperucita, anda visita a la abuela, que está enferma, y llévale esta canasta de comida."

This time, the entire target verbs were all underlined, bolded and in a larger font. The verbal morphology was then bolded. Which version do you prefer? Can you think of other ways of enhancing this text?

As you can see, there are many different ways to enhance target forms in a text. You need to carefully consider what is the best way to carry out the enhancement so that the form-function-meaning relationship associated with the form is as clear and as salient as possible. You may find it necessary to experiment with different alternatives in order to arrive at the best enhancement possible for a particular form. Don't be afraid to enlist the help of colleagues and perhaps even some students to help them determine what the best type of enhancement is for a given form. Experiment with a few different versions and ask colleagues and students what they think. Never hesitate to pilot materials before using them in class.

Remember to Keep Meaning in Focus

Remember that learners need to focus on meaning when they are reading the enhanced input. In order for form-meaning connections to be possible, learners must attend to both meaning and form. Recall also that there is a potential for textual enhancement to detract learners' attention from meaning. To minimize the chances of this happening, make sure that learners are pushed to attend to meaning. In other words, make sure learners have a reason for attending to the meaning. Ask yourself "What are learners going to do after they read the text?" Will they have to follow directions or perform some kind of action? Will they answer questions about the text? Will they take a test on the information? The point here is that we don't just enhance forms in written input and then throw it at the students. Learners need to be actively engaged in processing that input and respond to it in some way.

SUMMARY/CONCLUSION

As this chapter has demonstrated, textual enhancement can be a useful tool to help draw learners' attention to specific forms in written input. It is easy to implement and involves the use of meaning-bearing input, an essential ingredient to SLA. Research on textual enhancement shows that this technique may be effective in helping learners notice enhanced forms and in some cases, also make form-meaning connections from the enhanced input so that they are eventually able to use the forms in production. In the next chapter, we will talk about a type of input enhancement that is designed to make sure that the necessary form-meaning connections are actually happening. This technique is called "structured input."

ENHANCE YOUR KNOWLEDGE

L2 Textual Enhancement

Alanen, R. (1995). Input enhancement and rule presentation in second language acquisition. In R. Schmidt (Ed.), Attention and awareness in foreign language acquisition (pp. 259–302). Honolulu: University of Hawaii.

Jourdenais, R., Ota, M., Stauffer, S., Boyson, B & Doughty, C. (1995). Does textual enhancement promote noticing? A think-aloud protocol analysis. In R. Schmidt (Ed.), Attention and awareness in second language learning (Technical Report 9) (pp. 183–216). Honolulu: University of Hawaii, Second Language Teaching and Curriculum Center.

Leow, R. (1997). The effects of input enhancement and text length on adult L2 readers' comprehension and intake in second language acquisition. *Applied Language Learning, 8,* 151–182.

Leow, R. (2001). Do learners notice enhanced forms while interacting with the L2?: An online and offline study of the role of written input enhancement in L2 reading. *Hispania, 84,* 496–509.

Overstreet, M. (1998). Text enhancement and content familiarity: The focus of learner attention. *Spanish Applied Linguistics, 2,* 229–258.

Overstreet, M. (2002). *The effect of textual enhancement on second language learner reading comprehension and form recognition.* Unpublished doctoral dissertation, University of Illinois at Urbana-Champaign.

Shook, J. D. (1994). FL/L2 reading, grammatical information, and the input to intake phenomenon. *Applied Language Learning, 5,* 57–93.

Shook, J. D. (1999). What foreign language reading recalls reveal about the input-to-intake phenomenon. *Applied Language Learning, 10*, 39–76.

Simard, D. (2001). Effet de la mise en évidence textuelle sur l'acquisition de différente marques du pluriel en anglais langue seconde auprès de jeunes francophones de première secondaire. Doctoral dissertation, Université Laval, Québec.

White, J. (1998). Getting the learners' attention: A typographical input enhancement study. In C. Doughty & J. Williams (Eds.), Focus on form in second language classroom acquisition (pp. 91–128). Cambridge, MA: Cambridge University Press.

Wong, W. (2002b). *Decreasing attentional demands in input processing: A textual enhancement study.* Paper presented at the annual meeting of the Second Language Resarch Forum (SLRF), Toronto, Canada. October 3–6, 2002.

Wong, W. (2003). Textual enhancement and simplified input: Effects on L2 comprehension and acquisition of non-meaningful grammatical form. *Applied Language Learning, 13*, 109–132.

Historical Overview of Textual Enhancement

Simard, D. (2002). La mise en evidence textuelle: D'où venons-nous et où allons-nous? *Canadian Modern Language Review/La revue canadienne des langues vivantes, 59*, 236–263.

CHAPTER 6

Structured Input Activities

WHAT IS STRUCTURED INPUT?

The word *structured* is a common everyday term. For example, we have probably heard people speak of their day as being "structured." What does this mean? Does this mean that their day is haphazard or does it mean that they have a schedule that is organized and planned in some way? What about if they have a vacation that is structured? Does this mean that they just wake up everyday and go with the flow or would they have a carefully planned itinerary with specific activities to do each day? The typical meaning, of course, is that their days are planned and organized. But note something important about these terms, structured", "organized" and "planned" in our examples. These terms imply that the structure, plans or organization were imposed by someone, not that the person's day just happens to be structured. In order for our day or vacation to be structured, we must purposefully structure the day. Why would we want to do this? Most probably so that we could get certain things done or meet some goal. For example, in order for me to get this book done, I had to set up a structured schedule to help me meet my deadlines.

In the context of language acquisition, we may also speak of input as being structured. **Structured input** is input that has been structured to meet a particular goal. Lee and VanPatten (1995, 2003) call activities that use this type of input **structured input activities.** The goal of structured input activities is not just to get learners to notice target forms but to also alter any incorrect strategies they may be using to process input so that they can make form-meaning connections correctly and more efficiently. How do we do this?

How Are Structured Input Activities Carried Out?

Structured input activities are based on information about how learners make form-meaning connections. As you may recall from Chapter 3, this is also known as **input processing.** In order to change a faulty strategy, we

TABLE 6.1 Principles of VanPatten's Model of Input Processing

Principle 1 (P1). The Primacy of Meaning Principle. Learners process input for meaning before they process it for form.

P1a. The Primacy of Content Words Principle. Learners process content words in the input before anything else.

P1b. The Lexical Preference Principle. Learners will tend to rely on lexical items as opposed to grammatical form to get meaning when both encode the same semantic information.

P1c. The Preference for Nonredundancy Principle. Learners are more likely to process nonredundant meaningful grammatical form before they process redundant meaningful forms.

P1d. The Meaning-before-Nonmeaning Principle. Learners are more likely to process meaningful grammatical forms before nonmeaningful forms irrespective of redundancy.

P1e. The Availability of Resources Principle. For learners to process either redundant meaningful grammatical forms or nonmeaningful forms, the processing or overall sentential meaning must not drain available processing resources.

P1f. The Sentence Location Principle. Learners tend to process items in sentence initial position before those in final position and those in medial position.

Principle 2 (P2). The First Noun Principle. Learners tend to process the first noun or pronoun they encounter in a sentence as the subject or agent.

P2a. The Lexical Semantics Principle. Learners may rely on lexical semantics, where possible, instead of word order to interpret sentences.

P2b. The Event Probabilities Principle. Learners may rely on event probabilities, where possible, instead of word order to interpret sentences.

P2c. The Contextual Constraint Principle. Learners may rely less on the First Noun Principle of preceding context constrains the possible interpretation of a clause or sentence.

Source: Lee and VanPatten (2003)

must first understand what those less-than-optimal strategies are. Imagine that you are sick and you go to the doctor for medicine. Before the doctor can give you medicine to help you feel better, she needs to first find out what is wrong. The same goes for structured input activities. Before we can create an activity to remedy a particular processing problem, we first need to understand why the learner has difficulty making a particular form-meaning connection.

How do we find out this information? A lot of research has been conducted to find out what strategies learners use to pay attention to input and why. You will find a list of this research at the end of this chapter. This body of research led VanPatten to formulate what is known as a model of input processing. VanPatten's model contains a set of principles and subprinciples to describe the strategies that learners use to make form-meaning connections from input (see Table 6.1). This model serves as a guide to assist in the creation of structured input activities.

The first principle and subprinciples of the model are based on an understanding that learners are driven to get meaning from the input. What this means is that when learners hear a piece of input, they first try to understand the message the input conveys before paying attention to how that message is encoded linguistically. This is what VanPatten means when he says that learners will process input for meaning before form. He means that more meaningful items in the input will get processed before less meaningful ones. What are the more meaningful items in input? Content words. **Content words** are things in the input that carry the most meaning. For example, in the sentence *The apples are in the basket* which words are content words? If you said *apples* and *basket* you are correct. Content words are big words that have concrete meaning. Other examples of content words are *cat, dog, run, ball, Jane, she.* Subprinciple P1a states that content words are probably the first things that learners process. The subprinciples go on to explain that if a lexical item and a grammatical form both encode the same semantic information (or meaning), the learner will process the lexical item before the grammatical form (see P1b). What is a lexical item? A lexical item is any free standing unit of meaning. For example, *cat* can stand alone and means "feline." The *-s* of *cats* means "more than one" but cannot stand alone. *Cat* is a lexical item, *-s* is not. Thus, we can say that content words (e.g., *cat*) are also lexical items. However, not all lexical items are content words. The definite article *the* is a lexical item indicating "definiteness, a particular one" but it is not a content word like *cat*. *Cat* is a content lexical item, *the* is not. Note the difference: *The cat is on the mat.* vs. *Cat on mat.* vs. *The on mat.* Which of the latter two sentences is most likely to be interpreted first?

Let's try another example. Consider the following sentence:

Last night Ann watched TV.

If learners wanted to determine the temporal reference or tense of this sentence, which element in that sentence would they pay attention to first according to Principle 1? If you said *last night* you are correct. The words *last night* are content lexical items that tell us that the action took place in the past. What else in that sentence tells us that the action took place in the past? If you said the *-ed* on the end of the verb watch, you are right again. *-ed* is a morphological form that also expresses pastness. However, when learners are confronted with the above sentence, they would most likely pay attention or process the content lexical items *last night* before the morphological form *-ed* in the verb *watch* because the content lexical items carry more meaning.

Pause to consider . . .

what learners process in input. Which items do you think learners will notice and process first in the following sentences? Which items might they skip over?

1. My cat killed a squirrel yesterday.
2. There are some sodas on the counter in the kitchen.
3. Moths like to hide in dark places like my closet.

An important construct for understanding the first principle of VanPatten's model is the idea of communicative value. In Chapter 5 when we talked about Shook's textual enhancement study, we said that communicative value refers to the meaning that a form contributes to the overall meaning in a piece of input. We will elaborate on this here and add that **communicative value** is based on two features: +/−inherent semantic value and +/−redundancy. When we say that a form has **inherent semantic value,** we mean that the form has some kind of inherent meaning. Going back to our previous example sentence, we can say that the *-ed* in the verb *watched* has inherent semantic value because it expresses the meaning of pastness. An example of a form that does not have inherent semantic value is third person singular *-s* as in *he speaks.* The *-s* does not have inherent semantic value because it does not express any meaning.

Pause to consider . . .

forms that do not have inherent semantic value. Can you think of other examples of forms that do not have inherent semantic value?

Redundancy refers to whether the information carried in the form is also expressed elsewhere in a sentence or utterance. Let's go back to our sample sentence:

Last night Anne watched TV.

Would you say the form *-ed* in the verb *watch* is redundant or not redundant? If you said redundant, you are correct. Why? The *-ed* encodes the meaning of pastness and the idea of pastness is already expressed by the content words *last night.*

Any given form can have +semantic value and −redundancy, +semantic value and +redundancy, −semantic value and +redundancy, and −semantic value and −redundancy. VanPatten says that a form's communicative value is higher if it has the characteristics +semantic value and −redundancy than if it has the features +semantic value and +redundancy. Can you guess why? If you can get the referential meaning of a piece of input from something other than from the form in question itself, then the communicative value of that form would be diminished, right? In our sample sentence, the communicative value of the form *-ed* is diminished because we can get the concept of pastness (which the *-ed* encodes) from the content words *last night.* Now watch what happens when we remove *last night* from the input. We are left with the following:

Anne watched TV.

What happened here? We just made the communicative value of *-ed* higher because learners can no longer rely on *last night* to get the temporal reference of this sentence. They *have to* rely on *-ed* for this information. Can you see how we just structured the input so that the *-ed* is no longer redundant and takes on a higher communicative value? Learners can no longer rely on content words as a strategy to get tense from the sentence.

As you can see, redundancy is not absolute. Whether a form is redundant or not depends on the presence of other items in the input. Forms that are not redundant have higher communicative values. The higher the communicative value of the form, the more likely learners will pay attention to it and make form-meaning connections from it (P1c and P1d).

Pause to consider . . .

increasing the communicative value of forms. How could you increase the communicative value of the bolded forms in the following sentences?

1. Jane has **three** apples.
2. Yesterday I talk**ed** to my professor.
3. I prefer that you **be** on time.

What happens to forms that do not have inherent semantic value? When a form has semantic value, it has no communicative value regardless of the presence or absence of redundancy. According to VanPatten, forms of low or no communicative value tend to be processed much later or perhaps not at all.

Subprinciple P1e says that learners can only process forms of lower communicative value if they do not have to struggle with understanding the meaning of the message. If comprehension is difficult, they will not have any attentional resources left over to allow them to pay attention to form. However, if the message is comprehensible, there is a greater chance (but still no guarantee) that they will also be able to attend to form. This is why it may be better to give learners (especially beginning learners) sentence-level input before requiring them to process discourse-level input. Because short sentences are easier to process than connected discourse, learners will be more likely to pay attention to the relevant grammatical information that is the target of instruction. Wong's (2002b) study on textual enhancement discussed in Chapter 5 supports this principle. Wong found that learners who received sentence-level input performed better on an assessment task of the target structure (i.e., prepositions with geographical locations) than those who received discourse-level input.

Subprinciple P1f deals with how the position of a form may have an effect on whether or not it is likely to get processed. Consider the following examples:

1. People say that in Toronto you can find a lot of authentic Chinese restaurants.
2. In Toronto, you can find a lot of authentic Chinese restaurants.

In which sentence is the preposition *in* the most salient? If you said the second sentence, you are correct. In the second example, *in* is in initial position which makes it more salient. Research has shown that forms that are in initial position tend to be easiest to notice followed by forms in final position. Forms in medial position, as shown in the first sentence, tend to be the most difficult to notice and process.

Pause to consider . . .

the position of forms. In which version are past tense verbs more salient? Why?

1. Last night I came home late. I made my wife angry because I was late for dinner and I forgot to pick up the dry cleaning. I ate my dinner in silence and then apologized to my wife.
2. Last night I . . .

   came home late.

   made my wife angry.

   ate my dinner in silence.

   apologized to my wife.

The second principle is also known as the first noun principle. This principle deals with how word order can affect how learners process input. A common word order in some languages such as English is subject-verb-object (SVO). However, some languages such as Spanish do not follow this word order. In the following sentence in Spanish, the first noun-phrase the learner encounters is not a subject but learners who are used to an SVO word order may very well attempt to encode it as such:

La vio Juan en la fiesta anoche. (OVS)

her (object)   saw Juan (subject)   at the party last night

Juan saw her at the party last night.

Research has shown that when learners are confronted with such sentences, they have a tendency to encode such pronouns and noun phrases as subjects. When this happens, they deliver wrong intake data to their developing linguistic system. As you can see, in this case, it is not that meaning is being derived from a lexical item or another form in the utterance. Meaning is not gotten at all or is gotten wrong.

The subprinciples of Principle 2 point out that while learners have a tendency to rely on word order to interpret sentences or utterances, sometimes they may rely on other cues as well. These cues include lexical semantics (P2a), event probabilities (P2b) and context (P2c). Let's look at the following example in French.

Candice fait laver la voiture à Florian.

(lit. Candice makes to wash the car to Florian.)

Candice makes Florian wash the car.

According to Principle 2, a learner of French would incorrectly think that Candice washes the car rather than Florian because Candice is the first noun they see in the sentence. There are no other cues in the sentence to make them think otherwise. This is not the case with the next example:

> *Le professor fait faire les devoirs aux étudiants.*
>
> (lit. The professor makes to do the homework to the students.)
>
> The professor makes the students do the homework.

In this example, when asked who does homework, learners of French will likely say the students do. Does this mean that they processed the syntactic structure of the sentence correctly? Not necessarily. Unlike the first example where either Candice or Florian could have performed the action, there are lexical and contextual cues in this second example that limit the action of *doing homework* to the students. In the context of professors and students, it is typically professors who make students do homework and not the other way around. Thus, based on event probabilities and students' background knowledge about professors and students, learners might be able to interpret the sentence correctly even though they did not process the syntactic structure of the sentence correctly. According to VanPatten, when such cues are present, learners may abandon the first noun principle and rely on these cues instead.

Pause to consider . . .

word order as a processing problem. Can you think of any examples in the language that you teach where word order might interfere with how learners process that form?

To summarize, VanPatten's model of input processing describes how learners process input or how they make form-meaning connections from input. The principles and subprinciples in the model explain what features of input learners tend to pay attention to, which features they tend not to attend to and why.

How Do We Create Structured Input Activities?

Structured input activities are informed by the strategies that learners use to process input. Before we can begin to create a structured activity for a particular grammatical form, we must first understand what strategy learners are using to process that form. Then, and only then, can we structure the input so that learners abandon their inefficient strategies for more optimal ones. So before you design an activity, you need to ask yourself "What is the problem here?" Are learners relying on content words to get meaning instead of form? Is the problem due to an unfamiliar word order? Is it because the position of the form is not salient?

Let's say our learners are having difficulty processing the simple past tense form *-ed* in English. Using the model of input processing as a guide, what strategy or strategies would you say learners rely on to process this form? The answer is Principle 1. As we saw earlier, the idea of pastness can be encoded by temporal adverbs (content words) and by morphological forms. According to

Principle 1, learners will pay more attention to the content words for this information and consequently, may miss the *-ed* form. What we want to do in our activities is structure the input so that learners *must* pay attention to the form instead of the temporal adverbs to get the meaning of pastness. In other words, we don't want them to rely on content words as a strategy. We want to push them to pay attention to the form. Here is an example of what a structured input activity for this form may look like.

You will hear sentences that describe activities that Claude did yesterday or activities that he will do tomorrow. Listen carefully to the verbs in order to determine whether the action happened yesterday or will happen tomorrow. Claude . . .

1. a. yesterday   b. tomorrow
2. a. yesterday   b. tomorrow
3. a. yesterday   b. tomorrow

Instructor's Script:
(Claude . . .)

1. talked to his mother.
2. walked his dog in the park.
3. will call his aunt Freida.

Follow up: Who did some of these activities last night? Raise your hand if you did this activity last night.

1. Who called their mothers?
2. Who walked their dogs in the park?
3. Who called their aunts?

Etc.

Can you see how we structured the input in this activity so that learners must pay attention to verb forms in order to determine the temporal reference of each sentence? Because we know that learners tend to rely on content words, in this case temporal adverbs, to get meaning, we removed the adverbs so that they must pay attention to form in order to get meaning.

There are actually two types of structured input activities: referential activities and affective activities. The above activity is an example of a referential activity. **Referential activities** require that learners pay attention to form in order to get meaning and have right or wrong answers so instructors can immediately check if learners are indeed making the correct form-meaning connections. Notice that these activities require learners to pay attention to both meaning and form in order to successfully complete them. Furthermore, processing form in this activity allows learners to achieve a communicative goal (i.e., finding out who did what last night). **Affective activities,** on the other hand, do not have a right or wrong answer. Instead, they require learners to express an opinion, belief or some other affective response as they are engaged in processing information about the real world. The following is an example of an affective activity for the same target form.

Read the following activities and check off the ones that you did last night. Last night I . . .

    watched TV.

    fixed myself a cocktail.

    cleaned up my room.

    invited friends over for dinner.

Now share your responses with a classmate. Did you do the same things last night?

Did you notice how the input is structured so that the form is in the most salient position possible? Affective activities work very well in communicative classrooms because they encourage learners to give and receive meaningful information. However, since referential activities allow instructors to assess whether students are making the correct form-meaning connections, it is recommended that instruction begin with those. The purpose of affective activities is to reinforce those connections by providing them with more opportunities to see or hear the form used in a meaningful context as well as to encourage them to respond to the content of the input. More examples of structured input activities are in the Appendix at the end of this book.

Pause to consider . . .

other processing problems. You have just seen an example of a processing problem that deals with Principle 1 of the model of input processing. Can you think of forms in the target language you teach that deal with the other principles in the model? How might you design a structured input activity for these forms?

You will notice that learners do not produce the target structure in structured input activities. This is because the purpose of these activities is to help learners process input or make form-meaning connections better. In order for learners to produce good output, they must first get good input so that they can make good form-meaning connections. For example, you cannot make a dry cake light and moist by beating a cake with a hammer. If you want a good cake (output), you must put in the proper ingredients (input). The same goes for output. If we want learners to eventually produce good output, we have to make sure they are first getting good input. If you would like to learn how to create structured output activities, see Lee and VanPatten's (1995, 2003) volume.

Pause to consider . . .

forced output. In traditional approaches to instruction, learners are often given an explanation of the target form and then immediately asked to produce the form via exercises that require them to manipulate uses of the form. Why might this not be very effective?

Do Structured Input Activities Work?

A great deal of research has been conducted to determine whether structured input activities are effective. Two of these studies will be discussed in detail here.

The first study that examined the use of structured input activities was VanPatten and Cadierno (1993). This study set out to compare an instructional treatment that uses structured input activities with a traditional type of instruction that includes the use of mechanical drills. The instructional treatment that used structured input activities was called Processing Instruction (PI) because this treatment was designed to push learners to use better processing strategies to process input. The target forms in this study were Spanish object pronouns and word order. Subjects in the PI group were first given explicit information about how object pronouns work in Spanish. They were also told that learners of Spanish have a tendency to think that the first noun they encounter is the subject. They were told that this is not an effective strategy because Spanish has a more flexible word order and the first noun is not always the subject. After receiving this information, the subjects engaged in a series of structured input activities that pushed them to interpret word order and object pronouns correctly. They were never required to produce the target forms.

Subjects in the traditional instruction (TI) group received an explanation of object pronouns (but no information about inefficient processing strategies) and then they were given mechanical, then meaningful, then communicative output drills. This sequence of drills is very common in foreign language textbooks. Mechanical drills do not require that learners pay attention to meaning in order to complete the drill. Meaningful drills require some attention to meaning but there is only one correct response and the response is often obvious to learners. The control group did not receive any instruction or practice.

Pause to consider . . .

the value of mechanical drills. Some argue that mechanical drills have no value for language instruction because they are devoid of meaning and only give learners practice in manipulating language forms (the research done on processing instruction, in fact, shows that this type of practice is unnecessary). Others argue that mechanical drills have psychological value for learners because they are easy to do and give learners a sense of accomplishment when they are done with them. Which of these positions do you agree with?

The researchers found that on an interpretation test that required subjects to select pictures that best corresponded to what they heard, the PI group made improvements while the TI and control group did not. On a production test that required subjects to complete sentences based on pictures that they saw, both the TI and PI groups made the same amount of improvement. The control group did not improve. When subjects were tested again one month later with these tests, the same results were found.

The researchers concluded that PI is more beneficial than TI because not only did subjects in the PI group make improvements in ability to interpret object pronouns, but their input processing of this structure resulted in some kind of change in their system that allowed them to access what they learned for production. This is an important finding because at no time during treatment did subjects in the PI group ever practice producing object pronouns. Yet on the production task, they were able to perform as well as subjects in the TI group who received lots of practice in producing this structure. The subjects in the TI group on the other hand, could not do the interpretation task. Their performance on this task was no better than those in the control group who received no instruction. Subjects in the TI group were only good at doing what they practiced doing during treatment. Similar results have been found with many other PI studies using different target structures and languages (e.g., Cadierno, 1995; Cheng, 1995; VanPatten & Wong, 2004).

Pause to consider . . .

the evidence that mechanical drills are not necessary. How do the results of VanPatten and Cadierno's study show that mechanical drills are not necessary? Hint: Think of the results in terms of the types of practice that the PI group and the TI group received. Do you think instructors should give learners mechanical drills even if these drills are not necessary?

You may have noticed that the treatment in the PI group included both explicit information and structured input activities and may have said to yourself: "Could the superior results found for PI be due to the explicit information?" A study by VanPatten and Oikkenon (1996) set out to address this question and they found that the explicit information really did not help the subjects at all. They gave one group of subjects both explicit information and structured input activities. A second group received only the structured input activities and a third group received only the explicit information. These researchers found that the group that had both structured input activities and explicit information and the group that received only structured input activities made the same amount of improvement while the group that had only explicit information made no improvement at all. Can you see why this shows that the explicit information was not necessary? Had the explicit information been important, then the group that got both explicit information and structured input activities should have been better than the group that only got structured input activities. But this was not the case. The group that got only structured input activities was able to do just as well as the group that got both. This shows that the structured input alone was enough to push learners to change their processing strategies. Other studies that have found similar results include Benati (2004), Sanz and Morgan Short (2002), and Wong (2004).

Pause to consider . . .

the role of explicit information. VanPatten and Oikkenon found that explicit information was not beneficial in their study. The structured input activities alone were enough to push learners to make the correct form-meaning corrections. Can you think of some situations where explicit information might play a more beneficial role? Hint: think about the nature of some other input enhancement techniques. How is structured input different from these techniques?

What Are the Advantages and Disadvantages of Structured Input Activities in the L2 Classroom?

One of the most important advantages of structured input activities is that they are directly targeted at learners' processing strategies so there is a better chance that these activities will indeed help learners make the correct form-meaning connections. In fact, this is the only input enhancement technique that directly attempts to alter learners' processing strategies. Furthermore, there is a substantial amount of research to support that this technique is indeed effective.

Another advantage is that unlike input flood and textual enhancement where we can't be sure what learners notice and process, we can immediately check if learners are making the correct form-meaning connections with structured input activities. If learners do not make the appropriate form-meaning connections, they cannot successfully complete the activities.

Structured input activities are ideal for communicative language teaching classrooms because the activities encourage meaningful exchanges of information while requiring learners to pay attention to form at the same time. If instructors notice that their learners have trouble with a particular form, they could drop some structured input activities into their lesson to help learners process the form better.

A disadvantage of this technique is that structured input activities do require a lot of planning and thought. Any old input activity will not do. In order for the activity to be effective, the instructor must determine what inefficient strategy learners are using to process a particular form and then manipulate the input so that learners will be forced to use more optimal strategies. The results suggest, however, that they are well worth the effort.

How Do We Implement Structured Input Activities in the L2 Classroom?

Step 1: Identify the Processing Problem or Strategy

The first and perhaps most important step in developing structured input activities for the classroom is to identify and understand what the processing problem is for the form in question. Why are learners having problems processing a particular form? What strategies are they using that are causing them to process this form inefficiently or incorrectly? Is it due to a tendency to rely on lexical items (i.e., Principle 1)? Is it due to a word order problem (i.e., Principle 2)? Is the location of the form a problem (P1f.)? Or is some combination of factors involved? Remember that the goal of structured input is to push learners away from their less than optimal strategies for processing input. If the processing problem or strategy is not identified, we will not be able to create structured input activities to help reach this goal.

Step 2: Follow Guidelines for Developing Structured Input Activities

Once the processing problem has been identified, then the development of structured input activities can begin. The input in these activities should be structured so that learners cannot rely on inefficient strategies to successfully complete the activities. The activities should force them to use more optimal strategies to process the form in question. The following guidelines are adapted from Lee and VanPatten (1995, 2003). See also Wong (2002a, 2004a) for discussions on how to create structured input activities.

1. *Present one thing at a time.* This means that only one rule of usage and/or one form of a paradigm should be presented at a time. The reason for this guideline is simply this: when there is less to pay attention to, it is easier to pay attention.
2. *Keep meaning in focus.* You have heard this many times. In order for form-meaning connections to happen, learners must pay attention to both meaning and form. If the activity can be completed without attention to meaning, then it is not a structured activity.
3. *Move from sentences to connected discourse.* When we teach grammar via structured input activities, it is preferable to begin with sentences first because short sentences are easier to process than connected discourse. When comprehension is easy, learners will be more likely to pay attention to the relevant grammatical information that is the target of instruction.
4. *Use both oral and written input.* Both oral and written input should be used in structured input activities because learners should have opportunities to receive input in both modalities. While all learners need oral input, more visual learners would benefit from "seeing" the input as well. Not giving these learners exposure to written input could put them at a disadvantage in learning situations.
5. *Have learners do something with the input.* This guideline goes hand in hand with the goals of communicative language teaching. The activities should not only be meaningful, they should also be purposeful. This means that learners must have a reason for attending to the input. Therefore, the activities should have learners responding to the input in some way to ensure that they are actively processing the input.
6. *Keep the learner's processing strategies in mind.* This cannot be stressed enough. This guideline is in fact what distinguishes structured input activities from other input enhancement techniques. Remember that

the goal of these activities is to help learners move away from inefficient processing strategies so that they adopt more optimal ones.
Therefore, the processing strategies that learners use to process a
particular form must be kept in mind at all times in developing
structured input activities. If the activity is not constructed to correct
an inefficient processing strategy, then it is *not* a structured input
activity. This is why it is critical that the processing problem or the
processing strategies that learners use for a given form be clearly
identified *before* the activities are created.

Is There a Role for Explicit Information in Structured Input Activities?

As you saw in the research on Processing Instruction, learners were given
explicit information about the target form before they engaged in structured
input activities. This information was different from information used in other
types of instructional interventions because it included information about inefficient strategies that learners use to process a particular form. However, as we
saw from the research (e.g., VanPatten and Oikkenon), this information was not
necessary. Research shows that when done correctly, structured input activities
alone are sufficient to help learners make correct form-meaning connections
(at least for the target structures investigated so far). This is because structured
input activities work to alter inefficient or wrong processing strategies. Learners are required to make the correct form-meaning connections in order to
successfully complete the activities.

This of course does not mean that explicit information cannot be used with
structured input. Some learners are used to seeing this type of information and
may like to have it even if it is not necessary. The important thing to remember
is that it is the activity that will push the correct form-meaning connections, not
the explicit information.

SUMMARY/CONCLUSION

This chapter presented a type of input enhancement that alters how learners
process input so that they make better form-meaning connections. Structured
input activities are directly based on the strategies that learners use to process
input. To our knowledge, this is the only input enhancement technique that
makes use of such information. This information is important because the more
we know about what learners do with input, the better we will be at helping
them process input better. Because structured input activities are designed with
learners' processing strategies in mind, they probably stand the most chance at
altering learners' inefficient strategies so that optimal input processing can take
place. I have said elsewhere that creating activities without first identifying a
processing strategy is like a doctor passing out medication without knowing
what is wrong with the patient. Sometimes it may work and sometimes it won't
but we won't know why. With structured input activities, the doctor (instructor)
always knows why.

Creating Structured Input Activities

Lee, J., and VanPatten, B. (1995). *Making communicative language teaching happen*. New York: McGraw Hill.

Wong, W. (2002a). Linking form and meaning: Processing instruction. *The French Review, 76,* 236–264.

Wong, W. (2004a). The nature of processing instruction. In B. VanPatten (Ed.), *Processing Instruction: Theory, research and commentary*. Mahwah, NJ: Erlbaum.

Research on Structured Input Activities

Benati, A. (2001). A comparative study of the effects of processing instruction and output-based instruction on the acquisition of the Italian future tense. *Language Teaching Research, 5,* 95–127.

Cadierno, T. (1995). Formal instruction in processing perspective: An investigation into the Spanish past tense. *The Modern Language Journal, 79,* 179–194.

Cheng, A. (1995). *Grammar instruction and input processing: The acquisition of Spanish* ser *and* estar: Unpublished doctoral thesis, University of Illinois at Urbana-Champaign.

VanPatten, B. & Cadierno, T. (1993). Explicit instruction and input processing. *Studies in Second Language Acquisition, 15,* 225–243.

VanPatten, B. and Fernández, C. (2004). Longitudinal effects of processing instruction. In B. VanPatten (Ed.), *Processing Instruction: Theory, research and commentary*. Mahwah, NJ: Lawrence Erlbaum.

VanPatten, B. and Oikkenon, S. (1996). Explanation vs. structured input in processing instruction. *Studies in Second Language Acquisition, 18,* 495–510.

VanPatten, B. & Sanz, C. (1995). From input to output: Processing instruction and communicative tasks. In F. Eckman, D. Highland, P. Lee, J. Mileham, & R. Rutkowski Weber (Eds.), *Second Language Acquisition Theory and Pedagogy* (pp. 169–185). Mahwah, NJ: Erlbaum.

VanPatten, B. and Wong, W. (2004). Processing instruction and the French causative: a replication. In B. VanPatten (Ed.), *Processing Instruction: Theory, research and commentary*. Mahwah, NJ: Erlbaum.

Wong, W. (2004b). Processing Instruction in French: The role of explicit information and structured input. In B. VanPatten (Ed.), *Processing Instruction: Theory, research and commentary*. Mahwah, NJ: Erlbaum.

Research That Show Explicit Information Is Not Necessary

Benati, A. (2004). The effects of structured input activities and explicit information on the acquisition of Italian tense. In B. VanPatten (Ed.), *Processing Instruction*. Hillsdale, NJ: Erlbaum.

Sanz, C. and Morgan-Short, K. (2002). *Must computers deliver explicit feedback?* An Empirical Study. Paper delivered at the conference on Form-meaning

Connections in Second Language Acquisition. Chicago, February 21–24, 2002.

VanPatten, B. and Oikkenon, S. (1996). Explanation vs. structured input in processing instruction. *Studies in Second Language Acquisition, 18*, 495–510.

Wong, W. (2004b). Processing Instruction in French: The role of explicit information and structured input. In B. VanPatten (Ed.), *Processing Instruction: Theory, research and commentary.* Mahwah, NJ: Erlbaum.

CHAPTER 7

Grammar Consciousness-Raising Tasks

WHAT ARE GRAMMAR CONSCIOUSNESS-RAISING TASKS?

The term "consciousness-raising" generally means to heighten someone's awareness about something. In the field of SLA, consciousness-raising was a term first introduced by Rutherford and Sharwood Smith (1985) to refer to external attempts to draw L2 learners' attention to formal properties of a target language. As you may recall, Sharwood Smith later changed this term to "input enhancement" to emphasize the point that external efforts to get learners to pay attention to form does not guarantee that they actually will pay attention.

Grammar consciousness-raising (GCR) tasks as an input enhancement technique, may be attributed to the work of Ellis and Fotos. The goal of **grammar consciousness-raising tasks** is to make learners aware (or conscious) of the rules that govern the use of particular language forms while providing them with opportunities to engage in meaningful interaction. In other words, these tasks seek to help learners develop explicit knowledge about how the target language works and to push them to negotiate meaning. These tasks are based on the theoretical premise that explicit knowledge about how a particular grammar structure works will help learners notice that form in subsequent communicative input (e.g., Ellis, 1990; Fotos, 2002) and that interaction is essential to language acquisition (e.g., Ellis, 1992, 1997; Nunan, 1993). As noted by Long and Porter (1985) and Pica (1987), the use of tasks and group work that require the negotiation of meaning can expose learners to greater quantities of comprehensible input. Additionally, the interaction that takes place in tasks tend to push learners to make more adjustments in their own output.

It is important to point out that in GCR tasks, students are not given explicit information about the L2. Instead, they are encouraged to discover the rules on their own by performing an interactive task with input. Ellis (1997) defines consciousness-raising tasks as the following: "A [GCR] task is a pedagogic activity where the learners are provided with L2 data in some form and required to perform some operation on or with it, the purpose of which is to arrive at an explicit understanding of some linguistic property or properties of the target language" (p. 160).

How Are Grammar Consciousness-Raising Tasks Carried Out?

Before describing how to create a GCR task, it would be helpful to first make a distinction between this type of task and other task types. There are tasks that require learners to use the target structure in order to complete the task content, such as those advocated by Loschky and Bley-Vroman (1990). For example, the following task might be designed to induce learners to use the past tense—learners must guess what their teacher did last night after class and then compare their guesses with another student to see if they share the same perceptions about their teacher. As you can see, the content of the task (i.e., students' perceptions of their teacher based on what they think the teacher did last night) requires that learners use the past tense to complete the task, even if they may not use past tense forms correctly 100% of the time. Other tasks, such as the ones proposed by Ur (1988), actually require accurate production of the target form.

What makes GCR tasks different from these other task types is that first, the content of the task is the grammar itself. In GCR tasks, the topic of discussion is always grammar. Second, learners are not ever required to actually produce the target structure. Learners certainly could produce the structure while they are engaged in the interaction but the task itself does not require them to do so. Like all the input enhancement techniques treated in this book, the goal of GCR is to get learners to pay attention to the form, not make them able to immediately use the form:

> . . . the grammar consciousness-raising task is not aimed at developing immediate ability to use the target structure but rather attempts to call learner attention to grammatical features, raising their consciousness of them, and thereby facilitating subsequent learners [sic] noticing of the features in communicative input.
>
> —Fotos, 1994, p. 326

The rationale is that once consciousness about a particular grammatical form has been raised, then learners may be more likely to notice it in subsequent communicative input which could perhaps lead to the eventual acquisition of that feature (Ellis, 1990; Fotos, 2002).

In a GCR task, the grammar problem is typically in the form of a series of correct and incorrect sentences designed to help learners see the underlying rule behind the correct use of the particular grammatical structure. Here is an example of a GCR task taken from Simard and Wong (2004b), developed based on the original activities of Fotos and Ellis, focusing on the use of the indefinite articles *a/an:*

Instructions to students: In teams you are to study correct and incorrect sentences using the indefinite article *a/an*. You all have different sentences. You must read your sentences to your partner. Do not show your sentences to your partner. Only read the sentences as many times as necessary. Work together and decide on the basis of correct and incorrect sentences what form of the indefinite article should be used. Write the rule governing the form of the indefinite article. Choose one member from your pair to report the results to the rest of the class.

Student 1

1. Correct: There is an apple on the table.
1. Incorrect: There is a apple on the table.
2. Correct: An elephant is crossing the street.
2. Incorrect: A elephant is crossing the street.
3. Correct:T A boy is playing baseball.
3. Incorrect: An boy is playing baseball.

Student 2

4. Correct: There is a tree in our yard.
4. Incorrect: There is an tree in our yard.
5. Correct: An ostrich escaped from the zoo.
5. Incorrect: A ostrich escaped from the zoo.
6. Correct: My sister made a birthday cake.
6. Incorrect: My sister made an birthday cake.

As you can see, learners are required to work in pairs. Each person in the pair is given a portion of the sentences to read aloud to the other without showing the written sentences. As a pair, they need to decide on the basis of the correct and incorrect sentences they hear why the sentences are correct and incorrect and then write down the rule(s) that underlie the use of the target form. The need to come to a consensus about the rule(s) pushes learners to interact with one another. One person from each pair then reports the results to the rest of the class.

In this particular activity, learners are to work in pairs but it could easily be adapted for a small group by adding sentences and distributing the sentences differently. What is crucial here is that the sentences must be constructed in such a way so that learners are able to identify why a sentence is correct and incorrect. Thus, forms that can be directly contrasted and which have a clear rule appear to work best for such a task (such as with the indefinite articles a/an).

Pause to consider . . .

different target structures. Which target structures in the language that you teach may be good candidates for GCR tasks? Can you think of target structures that may not be ideal for this type of input enhancement?

Because the topic of discussion in GCR tasks is grammar, Fotos and Ellis (1991) advocate providing students with metalinguistic terminology if necessary. The following is an activity developed by Fotos and Ellis (1991) that focuses on the correct order of direct and indirect object pronouns in English. In addition to the metalinguistic terminology, they also developed a worksheet to help students discern which verbs allow certain orders of direct object pronouns.

Task Cards

Students in groups of 4—one different card to each member
Students in pairs—two different cards to each member

1. Correct:	I asked my friend a question.
1. Incorrect:	She asked a question to her mother.
2. Correct:	Kimiko reviewed the lesson for John.
2. Incorrect:	Kimiko reviewed John the lesson.
3. Correct:	The teacher calculated the answers for the students.
3. Incorrect:	The teacher calculated the students the answers.
4. Correct:	The secretary reported the problem to her boss.
4. Incorrect:	The student reported the teacher the matter.
5. Correct:	I offered her a cup of tea.
5. Correct:	I offered a cup of tea to the president.
6. Correct:	The teacher pronounced the difficult word for the class.
6. Incorrect:	The teacher pronounced the class the difficult word.
7. Correct:	I bought many presents for my family.
7. Correct:	I bought my family several presents.
8. Correct:	She cooked a delicious dinner for us.
8. Correct:	She cooked us a wonderful meal.
9. Correct:	She suggested a plan to me.
9. Incorrect:	She suggested me a good restaurant.
10. Correct:	The teacher repeated the question for the student.
10. Incorrect:	The teacher repeated the student the question.

Metalinguistic Information Sheet

There are some verbs in English which can have two objects. One of the objects is called the *direct object*. The other is called the *indirect object*. An indirect object names the person for whom the action of the verb is performed.

		(indirect object)		(direct object)
She	wrote	Susan	a	letter.

Different verbs may have the objects in different order, and this is often a problem for students of English. The following exercises will help you understand some confusing verbs.

Directions: In groups, you are to study correct and incorrect sentences using different verbs. You all have different sentences. You must read your sentences to the rest of the group. Do not show your sentences to the other members! Only read the sentences as many times as necessary! Work together as a group and decide on the basis of the correct and incorrect sentences where the direct and indirect objects should be located. Fill out the rest of this page. Choose one student to report your results to the rest of the class. Please speak only in English during this exercise!

Verbs   Possible correct order of direct and indirect object

1. asked: _____
2. reviewed: _____
3. calculated: _____
4. reported: _____
5. offered: _____
6. pronounced: _____
7. bought: _____
8. cooked: _____
9. suggested: _____
10. repeated: _____

Conclusion: Write 3 rules concerning the possible order of objects

Rule 1: _____
Verbs which follow this rule: _____
Rule 2: _____
Verbs which follow this rule: _____
Rule 3: _____
Verbs which follow this rule: _____

As you can see from this task, metalinguistic terminology is provided as well as an exercise to help learners identify the rule but it is the learners themselves who must articulate the rule through studying the sentences and interacting with their partners or other members of their group.

Do Grammar Consciousness-Raising Tasks Work?

In addition to creating GCR tasks, Fotos and Ellis also tested these tasks in carefully designed empirical studies. In their research, they wanted to investigate whether GCR tasks were successful in helping learners notice target forms, whether these tasks promoted interaction in the L2, and whether these tasks were as effective as teacher-fronted grammar instruction, that is to say, instruction where the teacher gives the rule to the students. Fotos (1993, 1994) conducted a study with first-year Japanese university students learning English in order to try to answer these questions. Three intact classes were used each representing a different experimental group: a GCR task group, a teacher-fronted grammar lesson group, and a communicative task group that served as a control group. Fotos used three target structures in her study: adverb placement, indirect object pronoun placement, and relative clause use. Participants in the GCR task group and grammar lesson group were first given a pretest of the structures in the form of grammaticality judgment (i.e., they had to judge the correctness of sentences) and sentence-writing tests. Participants in the control group did not do these tests. During treatment, participants in the GCR task group were put into groups of four and worked on GCR tasks similar to the examples presented in the previous section of this chapter. They were never given any explicit information about the structures. They studied correct and incorrect sentences together and then articulated the rules. In the teacher-fronted grammar lesson group, the teacher wrote the correct and incorrect sentences on the board, asked the students if they thought each sentence was correct or incorrect and then gave learners the rule for each structure. The control group did communicative tasks that did not focus on grammar (consequently, there was no focus on the target structures). In order to see whether the activities in the two treatment groups were effective, participants in the GCR task group and the teacher-fronted grammar lesson group were given the same grammaticality judgment and sentence-writing tests again. These tests served as post–tests. Fotos compared the pretest and posttest scores of the GCR group and the grammar lesson group and found that both groups made similar gains in accuracy. This means that GCR tasks were effective and that these tasks are as good as teacher-fronted grammar lessons.

In order to address the question of whether GCR tasks help learners notice the target structures in subsequent communicative input, all participants were given noticing activities to do one and two weeks after the treatment. These noticing activities were in the form of reading passages and dictation exercises that contained the target structures. Participants were asked to underline any 'special use of English' that they noticed in these exercises (Fotos, 1993, p. 390). Noticing was thus defined here as underlining any of the target structures embedded in the exercises. Fotos found that about 50% of participants in the GCR task group underlined the target structures in the passages. However, none of the participants in either the grammar lesson group or the communicative task group underlined the targets. Based on these results, Fotos concluded that once consciousness of a form is raised via GCR tasks, learners may continue to notice them later when they encounter these forms in input.

In order to determine whether the interaction that takes place during GCR tasks is comparable to the amount of interaction that takes place in communicative tasks where the content is not grammar, Fotos (1993, 1994) and Fotos and Ellis (1991) compared the amount of talk produced via these two task types. Their results revealed that participants in both the GCR task and the non-grammar-based communicative task produced the same amount of talk. Thus, based on these positive research results, Fotos and Ellis conclude that GCR tasks may be viewed as good communicative activities because these tasks promote noticing, proficiency gains, and meaningful interaction (see Fotos 1993, 1994, and Fotos & Ellis 1991, for complete details of these studies).

What Are the Advantages and Disadvantages of Grammar Consciousness-Raising Tasks in the L2 Classroom?

The advantages of GCR tasks should be clear. GCR tasks help learners pay attention to grammatical forms that they may otherwise miss on their own and at the same time, provide opportunities for meaningful interaction. As we discussed in Chapter 3, in addition to input, attention and interaction are also important to SLA. Research by Fotos and Ellis also shows that once learners' consciousness is raised via these activities, they may continue to notice targets forms later in input on their own.

This technique appears to be especially advantageous in situations where **explicit knowledge** about a grammatical form may be desired. Recall that in the study conducted by Trahey and White (1993) in Chapter 4 on input flood, the researchers found that while flooding the input with the target forms helped learners know what the correct possible positions for adverbs were, this technique was not successful in helping them know which positions were not possible. The researchers concluded that in order to know what is not possible in input, learners may need to be explicitly given this information. GCR tasks may be used as an option to provide learners with this information. In a GCR task, learners are given information about what is possible (i.e., the correct sentences), also known as **positive evidence,** as well as what is not possible (i.e., the incorrect sentences), also known as **negative evidence.** However, unlike teacher-fronted grammar explanations, it is the learners themselves who must explain why. Therefore, in situations where learners may benefit from explicit knowledge about a grammatical form, GCR tasks may be a good option. This technique helps learners develop explicit knowledge about a form while engaging them in interaction and negotiation of meaning at the same time.

Pause to consider . . .

the nature of different grammatical forms. Besides adverb placement, what other grammatical forms might benefit from negative evidence or explicit knowledge?

It is important to point out, however, that the "input" learners receive in this technique is qualitatively different from those of other input enhancement techniques that we have seen so far in this book. Because correct and incorrect input sentences are directly contrasted, the input in GCR tasks tends to be always teacher-generated and generally limited to sentence-level input. Furthermore, we may not be able to really say that the input in these sentences is meaning-bearing because these sentences do not typically communicate any kind of message. Their purpose is to contrast correct forms with incorrect forms. When the L2 is used to illustrate a grammatical form rather than to communicate a message, we call this **language for display purposes.** A sentence such as *An elephant is crossing the street* and its incorrect counterpart *A elephant is crossing the street* does not communicate any kind of message to which learners are supposed to attend. The fact that the target language is being used for display purposes, however, is counterbalanced by the fact that learners are also required to negotiate meaning in this technique. In so doing, they may generate rich comprehensible input for others as well as for themselves. As noted by researchers such as Sharwood Smith (1991) and Farley (2000), output produced by a learner can become input for someone else. Thus, we may say that in GCR tasks, learners get meaning-bearing input via interaction with classmates while performing the grammar task. Furthermore, additional written or oral input that is communicative in nature may be supplemented along with the series of correct and incorrect sentences (see for example the activities in the Appendix) to ensure that learners are getting ample amounts of meaning-bearing input.

Pause to consider . . .

the input sentences in GCR tasks. Because the purpose of these sentences is to contrast correct and incorrect uses of a particular grammatical form, they do not typically communicate any kind of message to which learners are supposed to attend. Do you think these tasks could be modified so that the input that learners have to work with is meaning-bearing (i.e., communicative)?

A disadvantage that Fotos and Ellis point out is that this technique may not always be appropriate for beginning learners because these learners often lack the ability to discuss grammar in metalinguistic terms (1991, p. 623). When this is the case, learners have a tendency to rely on their L1 to complete the task. Another potential disadvantage is that some learners may find grammar as a topic dry. Because these tasks are grammar tasks, the content of discussion will always be grammar and some learners may find this monotonous. A follow-up activity that is not a grammar solving problem, perhaps, could help remedy this potential drawback.

Pause to consider . . .

the discussion of grammar. Do you think it is possible for learners to arrive at an understanding of the grammar rules that underlie a particular structure without using a lot of metalinguistic terminology? How might you design a grammar consciousness-raising task for beginning learners?

How Do We Implement Grammar Consciousness-Raising Tasks in the L2 Classroom?

Because GCR tasks are designed to help learners develop explicit knowledge about a particular grammatical structure, these tasks are ideal for language classes that use a **structural syllabus,** that is to say, a syllabus that is organized around specific grammar topics. Let's say that the grammar topic for Monday's class is adverbs. Learners could be asked to engage in a GCR task as a means of introducing this grammar topic. After consciousness has been raised for this grammar topic, the instructor may choose to follow up with a formal lesson on the topic if so desired and/or with additional communicative activities containing the form to encourage continued awareness of that grammatical form. You will see some examples of follow-up activities in the Appendix at the end of this book.

GCR tasks appear to be most ideal for a structural syllabus but there is no reason why they cannot also be integrated into classes that are not organized around grammatical topics, such as classes that use a functional syllabus. In a **functional syllabus,** classroom instruction is organized around different linguistic functions such as giving compliments or making a complaint. If, for example, the instructor notices that learners are having difficulty understanding a particular grammar point that is needed to fulfill a desired function, a GCR task for that grammatical form may be dropped in to raise learners' consciousness of that form. Once consciousness has been raised, the instructor may move on and continue with activities related to the functional topic of the day.

Pause to consider . . .

GCR tasks and classrooms that do not use a structural syllabus. Do you think it is possible to incorporate GCR tasks into a content-based classroom? How might this be done?

SUMMARY/CONCLUSION

In this chapter, I presented an input enhancement technique developed by Fotos and Ellis that aims at helping learners develop explicit knowledge about a particular grammatical form while providing learners at the same time with opportunities to engage in interaction and negotiation of meaning. This technique appears to be especially beneficial in situations where explicit knowledge about a particular form is desired or where negative evidence may be needed (as in the case with adverb placement in English) so that learners are aware of what is not possible in the target language. For instructors who are looking for acceptable ways to integrate explicit grammar instruction into communicative classrooms, this technique appears to be a good option. Because it is the learners themselves who must articulate the rules as they engage in these grammar problem-solving tasks, the classroom remains student-centered and conducive to meaningful interaction. As you may recall from Chapter 1, these characteristics are important tenets of communicative language teaching.

ENHANCE YOUR KNOWLEDGE

Grammar Consciousness-Raising Tasks

Fotos, S. (1993). Consciousness raising and noticing through focus on form: Grammar task performance vs. formal instruction. *Applied Linguistics, 14,* 385–407.

Fotos, S. (1994). Integrating grammar instruction and communicative language use through grammar consciousness-raising tasks. *TESOL Quarterly, 28,* 323–351.

Fotos, S. (2002). Structure-based interactive tasks for the EFL grammar lesson. In E. Hinkel and S. Fotos (Eds.), *New perspectives on grammar teaching in second language classrooms* (pp. 135–154). Mahwah, New Jersey: Erlbaum.

Fotos, S., & Ellis, R. (1991). Communicating about grammar: A task-based approach. *TESOL Quarterly, 25,* 605–628.

Fotos, S., Homan, R., & Poel, C. (1994). *Grammar in mind: Communicative English for fluency and accuracy.* Tokyo: Logos.

CHAPTER 8

Some Final Considerations

If I have accomplished the goal of this book, you should at this point be very familiar with the input enhancement techniques presented in this text: input flood, textual enhancement, structured input activities, and GCR tasks. You should understand why input is critical to SLA and see how these techniques may aid in the process of acquisition. You should understand that the motivation for input enhancement comes from the uncontested finding in SLA that learners must have access to ample amounts of comprehensible input in order for acquisition to be successful. You should see that the input enhancement techniques presented in this book have the advantage of drawing L2 learners' attention to grammatical form while also providing them with the input they need for acquisition.

In this final chapter, before offering some final thoughts, I will attempt to tie things together by addressing a few final points: (1) what we need to consider when making decisions about the type of input enhancement technique to use; (2) how these techniques may be integrated into different syllabus types; (3) how to assess whether these techniques have accomplished what they are supposed to, and finally (4) a few words about the role of output and other techniques.

HOW DO WE CHOOSE WHICH TECHNIQUE TO USE?

In the four chapters devoted to input enhancement techniques, we examined some research from SLA to give us some insight into the relative effectiveness of each technique. These experiments were conducted in highly controlled settings in order to isolate the effect of each technique from other variables that may impact the effect of instruction. As you know, in actual classroom settings, instructors are not limited to just one input enhancement technique. Instructors can and often do make use of many techniques at the same time (or at least in the same lesson) to respond to students' needs and interests. For example, technique A may be used to introduce a target form to learners, technique B may be used to encourage learners to make form-meaning connections, technique C may be used to provide additional opportunities for learners to notice the target form after form-meaning connections have been made, and perhaps technique B could be used again as a review, and so on. The combinations and possibilities are endless. The following are two general guidelines that I believe may help instructors decide which input enhancement technique may be optimal for different circumstances:

Consider the Nature of the Target Form

When selecting the type of input enhancement to use, it may be helpful to consider the nature of the target form in question. Because not all forms are created equal, some enhancement techniques may be more effective for certain forms over others. One question we may ask when considering the nature of a target form is the following: "How transparent is the form's form-meaning relationship?" You may recall that we have already examined the concept of transparent form-meaning relationships in Chapter 5 when we talked about textual enhancement. We will briefly revisit this concept here.

Again, by "transparent form-meaning relationship," I mean that the form in question has a distinct meaning or function that corresponds to it. We said in Chapter 5 that plural *-s* in English is an example of a structure that has a transparent form-meaning relationship because this form has a clear corresponding meaning distinction: *-s* expresses plurality (*dog* vs. *dogs*). Modal auxiliaries such as *may* or *might,* on the other hand, do not have a transparent form-meaning relationship because they do not have a distinct clear meaning distinction. For example, we use *may* to express possibility (*I may rent a video tonight*) but we also use it to express the idea of giving permission (*May I go to the bathroom?*). In Spanish, the choice of the copular verbs *ser* and *estar* is another example.

Pause to consider . . .

transparent form-meaning relationships. What forms in the language that you teach could be considered forms that have transparent form-meaning (or form-function) relationships? What forms do not have transparent form-meaning relationships?

With techniques that are more implicit in nature, such as input flood or textual enhancement, you will likely find that they will be more effective with forms that have a transparent form-meaning relationship. We said earlier that these techniques are implicit because other than embedding the form in the input, or in the case of textual enhancement, increasing its perceptual salience via typographical cues, nothing else is done to point out the form to the learner. Because learners will need to make correct form-meaning connections based on seeing or hearing input alone, the target form will need to have a form-meaning relationship that is fairly transparent in order for them to do so. Otherwise, they may not be able to comprehend the meaning that the form encodes, even if they do notice the form. Recall in our discussion in Chapter 3 that in order for learners to make form-meaning connections, they have to both notice and comprehend the form (i.e., the meaning it encodes). For target forms that have form-meaning relationships that are less transparent, techniques such as structured input or GCR tasks may be more efficient. Why? The nature of these techniques will likely be more effective in pushing learners to make the correct form-meaning connections. In GCR tasks, for example, learners are led to formulate the rules that underlie the use of a particular target structure. In this sense, we could say that learners are encouraged to make correct form-meaning connections. If they don't, they probably won't be able to come up with the correct rules. In structured input activities, learners are also pushed to make correct form-meaning connections. Recall that learners *must* notice and process the target forms in order to successfully complete the activity. Furthermore, structured input activities are designed to circumvent specific processing problems that learners encounter when they attempt to process certain grammatical forms. Thus, the best target forms for this technique will be those forms for which a processing problem or difficulty may be identified.

Keep in Mind the Goal of the Enhancement

We just said that input flood and textual enhancement are techniques that are best suited for target forms that have transparent form-meaning relationships. Does this mean that we should not use input flood or textual enhancement if the form we want to enhance does not have a transparent form-meaning relationship? The answer lies in what we would like the enhancement to do. Perhaps your lesson follows a presentation, practice and application sequence. For the presentation component of the lesson, it may not be necessary that learners make correct form-meaning connections right away. Maybe we just want to introduce or present the form used in context in some way. If this is our goal, then I would say that input flood and textual enhancement would be appropriate techniques, even if the form in question does not have a transparent form-meaning relationship. We could follow up during the practice portion of the lesson with either structured input activities or GCR tasks to increase the likelihood that learners will make correct form-meaning connections. Thus, it all depends on what the goal of the enhancement technique is.

What if the goal of instruction was to help learners have explicit or metalinguistic knowledge about the target structure? If you said GCR tasks, you are correct. Recall that GCR tasks are designed to help learners develop explicit knowledge about a particular grammatical form as they attempt to solve a grammar problem together. This technique would also be ideal in learning contexts where learners need to have negative evidence in order to know what uses of a form are not possible. Recall from our discussion in Chapter 4 on input flood that the provision of input can only tell us what is possible in an L2 but not what is NOT possible. By providing learners with examples of both correct and incorrect sentences, GCR tasks have the advantage of offering negative evidence to learners.

How Do We Integrate These Techniques into Different Types of Syllabi?

We have already discussed how each input enhancement technique may be used in the classroom in Chapters 4–7. Now I would like to look more closely at different types of syllabi that may be found in L2 classrooms and examine how input enhancement techniques may be integrated into these different types of classrooms.

Structural, Functional, Task-Based and Content-Based Instruction

Most L2 classrooms are organized around three types of syllabi: a structural syllabus (also known as grammatical syllabus), a functional syllabus or a task-based syllabus. I have already briefly discussed some of these in preceding chapters. I will do so again here for the sake of convenience.

In a **structural syllabus,** the syllabus is organized around different grammatical structures such as simple present tense verbs, regular past tense or the subjunctive form, and so on. A **functional syllabus** is not organized around grammatical structures but is instead organized around different linguistic functions that learners are expected to be able to perform in the L2. Giving compliments, complaining and expressing agreement/disagreement are all examples of the kinds of functions that L2 learner may be expected to perform in a class that uses such a syllabus. A **task-based syllabus,** as its name suggests, is organized around a series of tasks. The tasks may include things like conducting a survey, planning a dinner party, or deciding what clothing and equipment to buy for a special vacation.

Some classrooms use a content-based syllabus. In **content-based** instruction, the syllabus is not organized around grammatical structures, language functions or tasks. As you may recall from Chapter 1, students in content-based instruction classes learn academic subjects such as history, political science and biology in the L2. Thus, the L2 is the medium rather than the object of instruction.

Pause to consider . . .

input and types of classrooms. In which of the following classrooms is communicative input likely to be the most abundant: a structural-based classroom, a functional-base classroom, a task-based classroom or a content-based classroom? Why?

Can we use all the input enhancement techniques presented in this book with these different syllabus types? The answer is yes, but as you will see, the degree to which the technique may interrupt the normal instructional content of the class may vary.

Figure 8.1 illustrates how different input enhancement techniques may be integrated into different class types.

	Structural	Functional	Task-Based	Content-Based
Input Flood	X	X	X	X
Textual Enhancement	X	X	X	X
Structured Input	X	Drop in	Drop in	Drop in
GCR Task	X	Drop in	Drop in	Drop in

X = integration without interruption of content

FIGURE 8.1 Integration of input enhancement techniques by syllabus type.

As you can see, the implicit nature of input flood and textual enhancement allows these techniques to be smoothly integrated into all class types without interrupting the content of instruction. Let's say that an instructor of a task-based class notices that students are having difficulty with the subjunctive form in Spanish. The instructor in this case could flood the instructions for the tasks with the subjunctive form or perhaps give students texts to read that are related to the task at hand that contain multiple exemplars of the subjunctive form. Textual enhancement could also be used to increase the perceptual salience of the forms in the reading materials. In a content-based class, the instructor could simply incorporate textual enhancement into existing instructional materials to draw students' attention to target forms. Let's say you are teaching a content-based course on American history and you noticed that your ESL students tend to drop the *-s* on third person singular verb forms. To help your students pay attention to this form, you could highlight or underline the *-s* on all third person singular verb forms in their reading materials. Additional readings on American history could also be given to them that contain many uses of the target form. In a structural-based classroom, instructors could use input flood and textual enhancement to either present, to practice or to review the grammatical form that is the focus of instruction for the day.

Structured input activities and GCR tasks, on the other hand, are probably easiest to integrate into structural-based classrooms over other classroom types. Because a structural syllabus is organized around grammar topics, instructors could easily use structured input activities and GCR tasks to either present or practice the target grammatical structure designated on the syllabus that day. These techniques may also be used in classrooms that do not follow a structural syllabus, but the use of these techniques will likely interrupt the content of instruction, at least for a brief time. By interruption of content I mean that we would have to stop what we normally do in such classrooms to carry out the enhancement technique. For example, if instructors decided to use structured input activities or GCR tasks in a content-based class, they would probably have to "drop" them into a lesson plan as a special activity. Going back to our American history content class, if we wanted to use a structured input activity or GCR task to help our students pay more attention to third-person singular *-s*, then we would have to interrupt our history lesson in order to take time out to do these activities. We could perhaps have students do a GCR task before or after the history lesson of the day. We might also follow up the next class with a structured input activity on third person singular *-s* before starting the next history lesson.

Thus, it is certainly possible to use these techniques in classrooms that do not follow a structural syllabus, but we would need to be willing to accommodate the interruption that these techniques may bring into the classroom. Once awareness of a form is heightened and we are satisfied that our learners have made the correct form-meaning connections, we could move on and continue with our normal lesson.

Pause to consider . . .

structured input activities and GCR tasks. Do you think it is possible to design these activities in such a way so that they do not interrupt the regular content of classes that do not follow a structural syllabus? Could you design structured input activities and GCR tasks that could be integrated easily into a biology content class? What about for an algebra class?

How Do We Assess the Effectiveness of These Techniques?

We have talked about guidelines to consider when choosing an input enhancement technique and how these instructional interventions may be used in different types of classrooms. Now we need to ask the following: "How do we know that a technique has accomplished what it is supposed to?" To answer this question, we need to go back and think about the purpose of input enhancement.

Recall from Chapter 1 that Sharwood Smith says that the purpose of input enhancement is to make certain features of the L2 more salient so that learners will be more likely to pay attention to them. Paying attention to target forms is important because as we said in Chapter 3, only input that has been attended to and comprehended in some way can become intake for acquisition. Sharwood Smith also warned us that even when learners do pay attention to the target forms, there is no guarantee that they will internalize those forms. As we discussed in Chapter 2, acquisition is complex and slow and instructors cannot control what learners will process from L2 input. Furthermore, as Lightbown noted, comprehension tends to precede production. Therefore, we should not expect learners to be able to use target forms correctly in production immediately after an input enhancement technique has been administered. They certainly could but there is a good chance that they will not (at least not immediately).

Because input enhancement is presumed to increase the chance that learners will pay attention to the target form, we should expect them to notice the form and hopefully also comprehend the meaning that the form encodes so a form-meaning connection is made. There is never a guarantee that they will, but if they do, then we may say that our input enhancement technique has been effective. How do we know if learners have noticed a form or not? How do we know if they have made a form-meaning connection?

In SLA research, researchers design carefully controlled tasks to measure the construct of noticing. One such technique is called a think-aloud protocol. In this technique, learners are asked to verbalize their thoughts (think aloud) as they read a text or perform some other kind of task that contains the target structure and these verbalizations are tape-recorded. Each time the learners make a mention of the target structure, we say that the learner has "noticed" it (however, notice that this technique only tells us whether a form was noticed, it does not necessarily tell us whether a form-meaning connection was also made).

In the classroom, it is obvious that instructors cannot use techniques such as a think-aloud protocol to assess whether students have noticed a target form. How can instructors know that learners have noticed the target form in a particular input enhancement technique? Mentioning the form or using the form would certainly be evidence of noticing but as we said before, we cannot always expect learners to do this. Furthermore, not mentioning a form does not mean that learners have not noticed it. An alternative way for instructors to know whether learners have paid attention to a target form is to build "noticing" into an activity itself. Structured input, for example, is such an activity. Recall that these activities are designed so that learners *must* pay attention to the target form in order to get meaning from input. In order for learners to successfully complete structured input activities, they must have necessarily noticed the target form and made the correct form-meaning connection from the input (review the sample activities in Chapter 6 and the Appendix). If they have not, they cannot complete the activity (at least not successfully). Thus, we could say that assessment of noticing (and the creation of form-meaning connections) is inherent in structured input activities. Successful completion of an activity constitutes evidence that the learner has noticed the target forms and has made the correct form-meaning connection.

GCR tasks also have "noticing" built into activities. In GCR tasks, learners examine strings of correct and incorrect sentences and as a group or pair, have to articulate the rules that underlie the use of that target form. If learners can come up with the correct rule, then that is also evidence that they have noticed the target forms and have understood how the form works (you may want to review the sample activities in Chapter 7 and the Appendix).

This is not the case, however, with input flood and textual enhancement. With these techniques, we cannot tell from exposure to input alone that learners have actually noticed the target forms, even if those forms were enhanced through textual enhancement. Additionally, even if learners do notice the forms, we cannot tell if they also understand the meaning that the form encodes. In order to assess whether or not target forms were noticed in input flood and textual enhancement, we would need to give learners a task to do that would require them to notice the forms. In order to assess whether form-meaning connections were also made, the task would need to require them to comprehend the meaning that the form encodes. If you go back to the sample materials presented in Chapter 4 (input flood) and Chapter 5 (textual enhancement) as well as those in the Appendix, you will see that the follow-up activities often do require learners to notice target forms. Some of these "noticing" activities include:

- reading comprehension questions that require learners to pay attention to target forms and process them correctly in order to answer questions correctly;
- following a recipe;
- guessing whether statements made about a person are true or false.

Let's look at an example. Suppose our target forms are the possessive determiners *his* and *her* and we want to use textual enhancement to help learners notice these forms. We can give them the following text to read, an excerpt of a story adapted from Chinese mythology:

When Hou Yi reached **his** house, he stopped, and for safekeeping, he hid **his** magic pill in the straw-thatched roof. Then he went to share **his** joy with **his** wife who was sitting by the fire in **his** favorite chair. Chang E listened quietly as **her** husband told her of **his** plan to take the pill in twelve months. **Her** eyes became big like two apples. While **her** husband continued with **his** story, she thought to herself, "What about me? Why should I live like everyone else while my husband lives forever?"

As you can see, the target forms in the text are flooded and enhanced but how can we be sure that our learners have noticed the target forms and have made correct form-meaning connections? The answer is we cannot. In order for us to know this, we would have to give them a task that requires them to notice and process the possessive determiners correctly. What if we gave them the following comprehension questions to answer?

1. Whose chair was Chang E sitting in?
   a. Chang E's chair.
   b. Hou Yi's chair.
2. Whose eyes became big like apples?
   a. Chang E's
   b. Hou Yi's

Do we now have a way of knowing whether they noticed and processed the target forms correctly? The answer is yes. In order for learners to answer these questions correctly, they must have noticed and processed the possessive determiners correctly. They have to know that in the phrase *his favorite chair*, the chair must belong to a male, in this case, Hou Yi. They have to know that *her eyes* means that the eyes must belong to a female subject, in this case, Chang E. If learners said that b was the correct answer to the second question, then we would know that they did not make the correct form-meaning connection. Do you see how these comprehension questions allow us to assess the effectiveness of the input enhancement technique?

Again, if we wish to assess whether an input enhancement technique was effective or not and that technique does not have an assessment of noticing built in, we need to make sure that we include activities that require learners to notice the target forms. Otherwise, we will not know whether our input enhancement technique has accomplished what it was supposed to. Additionally, once we know that learners have noticed the target form, we also want to make sure that we provide them with additional opportunities to continue to notice the form in communicative input. As we said in Chapter 4 when we discussed input flood, the frequency of a form may have an impact on noticing (Gass, 1997). The more chances learners have to encounter a form in input, the more likely they are to notice it and perhaps process it for acquisition.

Pause to consider . . .

the assessment of input enhancement techniques. Do you think instructors should always assess whether or not an input enhancement technique was effective? Is it always necessary to do this?

What about Output?

This book has focused on the important role that input plays in SLA and instructional techniques that draw on the provision of input as their foundation for instruction. Before concluding, I would like to say a few words about output. First, I would like to point out that the fact that I have chosen to focus on input does not mean that I do not believe that output is important. Output is indeed also an important component of SLA but for different reasons. Swain provides a good summary of the roles that output plays in acquisition. It is not within the scope of this book to go into a detailed discussion about the role of output but I will highlight here a few points taken from Swain (1998):

- *Output promotes noticing of linguistic features in input.* When learners are forced to produce language, they may come to realize that they cannot say what they want to say. This in turn pushes them to search in the input for ways to express their meaning.
- *Output promotes hypothesis testing.* In this case, learners may hypothesize how to say something in a language but not be sure. They subsequently confirm or disconfirm their hypotheses via interaction with more input.
- *Output promotes conscious awareness of language and language use.* Heightened awareness in general may promote those processes that are responsible for acquisition.

As these points illustrate, output is something that promotes how learners interact with input for continued growth of their linguistic systems. VanPatten (2003) adds that output may help learners develop fluency. The more we practice accessing linguistic data from our implicit linguistic system, the more likely we are to develop fluency in the L2. However, output cannot replace input as the means by which acquisition takes place. In other words, output can be critical to stimulate acquisition processes, but it cannot replace them. Thus, output works at retrieving language data while input is responsible for getting that data into the system. Input is one piece of the puzzle and output is another. I have chosen to focus on the former. For readers who wish to read a non-technical account of the role of output in SLA, I refer them to Chapter 4 of VanPatten's (2003) volume, *From Input to Output: A Teacher's Guide to Second Language Acquisition.*

A Few Words about Other Techniques

This book has focused on instructional techniques that rely on the provision of input. Other pedagogical techniques that draw learners' attention to form include the Garden Path technique, dictogloss, and corrective feedback. In the **Garden Path technique** (Tomasello & Herron, 1989), the instructor purposely leads learners "down the garden path" to make errors and then subsequently draws their attention to the errors. In a **dictogloss** (Swain, 1998), the instructor reads a short, dense text to learners at normal speed. Learners jot down notes and then work together in pairs or groups to reconstruct the text using their shared resources. Dictoglosses are designed so that production of the target form is likely to occur. **Corrective feedback** involves pointing out to a learner that his or her use of the L2 is incorrect. **Recasts,** for example, are one type of corrective feedback. In this technique, when a learner makes an error, the instructor rephrases the learner's incorrect utterance correctly (e.g., Lyster, 1998). A discussion on how to help learners pay attention to form via output and other types of instructional techniques is the subject for another book. (See Chapter 10 in Doughty & Williams, 1998, for a more detailed discussion of these and other techniques).

FINAL WORDS

Once again, the instructional techniques presented in this book all share one common essential ingredient: input. These techniques rely on the provision of meaning-bearing input or primary linguistic data as their foundation for getting learners to notice target forms. As I first said in the preface of this book, I chose to focus on techniques that are input-based because input is an uncontested essential ingredient of SLA. I will borrow the words of Gass here once again: "The concept of input is perhaps the single most important concept of second language acquisition" (1997, p. 1). It is the gas that makes a car run. It is the yeast that makes bread rise. It is the water that makes plants grow. No one can learn a language without having access to input in some way.

When I reflect on the history of L2 instruction, I am struck by how far grammar instruction has come. Once associated with "the pedantic giving and testing of rules" (Sharwood Smith 1981, p. 160), we now have a wide array of options to help our language learners pay attention to grammatical form. As researchers continue to investigate the effects of L2 instruction and methodologists continue to improve teaching methods, new techniques will undoubtedly surface and we will know even more than we do today. One colleague joked that maybe we will have visually enhanced electronic texts where the target forms will pulsate or jump out at learners to grab their attention. Who knows? Maybe he's right. I am not going to try to predict what these new techniques will look like, but there is one thing that we can be sure of—input will remain an essential ingredient of successful SLA and L2 instruction. I know that will not change.

Sample Materials

A. INPUT FLOOD—SAMPLE MATERIALS FOR RUSSIAN

Target Structure: Future Tense Verb Forms

The bolding is for the benefit of the reader of this text only. Target forms are not usually visually enhanced in input flood. Note: This content may be modified for use in Spanish, English, French, Italian or German (among other languages).

Activity A. Mysterious Letter.[†] While investigating the murder of a Russian woman, the detective finds the following letter in the victim's apartment. The first paragraph of the letter appears to be missing. Read the letter and answer the questions that follow.

*Я уеду. Завтра же. **Перееду** в другой город, **поменяю** своё имя, **перекрашу** волосы. Я **стану** совершенно другим человеком. Ты не **узнаешь** меня. Никто не **узнает**. Я **начну** новую жизнь, **найду** новую работу, новых друзей. Моя жизнь постепенно **войдёт** в свою колею, и я **перестану** думать о тебе. И я **буду** счастлива.*

(Letter continues)

I **will** leave. Tomorrow even. I **will move** to another city, I **will change** my name, color my hair. I **will become** a completely different person. You won't recognize me. No one **will recognize** me. I **will start** a new life, find a new job, new friends. My life **will settle** down gradually, and I **will stop** thinking about you. And I **will be** happy.

Help the detective solve his case by answering the following questions:[‡]

1. *Что собирается делать автор этого письма?*
2. *Что, по-вашему, произошло между автором письма и адресатом?*
3. *Как, по словам автора, отреагирует адресат на её отъезд?*
4. *Будут-ли успешны его попытки? Да или нет? Почему?*

[†] Instructor's Note: This is a teacher-generated letter designed to expose learners to many uses of the future form in context.
[‡] Instructor's Note: These questions were created to encourage learners to pay attention to future tense forms in the letter they had to read.

5. *Какой совет даёт автор адресату?*
6. *Как вы думаете, может-ли адресат быть подозреваемым в деле об убийстве автора этого письма? Да или нет? Почему?*

1. What is the author of this letter planning to do?
2. What do you think happened between the author of the letter and its addressee?
3. According to the author, how will the addressee react to her leaving?
4. Will his attempts be successful? Yes or no? Why?
5. What advice does the author give to the addressee?
6. Do you think the addressee of this letter could be a suspect in the murder case? Why or why not?

B. TEXTUAL ENHANCEMENT—SAMPLE MATERIALS FOR ITALIAN

Target Structure: Adverbs

Note: This content may be adapted for use in virtually any language.

Segue una ricetta tipica della cucina italiana elaborata da Alessia. Leggere la ricetta e rispondere alle domande.

Tortelloni con ripieno di funghi porcini al tartufo nero

250g di tortelloni ai funghi porcini
1 tartufo nero (della grandezza di una noce)
2 cucchiai di panna da cucina
15g di burro
1 mazzetto di prezzemolo
1/2 bicchiere di latte
50g di parmigiano reggiano
1. Tritare **GROSSOLANAMENTE** il prezzemolo, unire una metà del tartufo tagliandolo **INTERAMENTE** a fettine sottilissime. 2. Frullare il tartufo restante e aggiungere il latte e **CONSEGUENTEMENTE** la panna. 3. Cuocere i tortelloni **RIGOROSAMENTE** al dente in abbondante acqua salata, scolare **BENE.** 4. Unire ai tortelloni il prezzemolo, il tartufo tagliato a fettine, gli ingredienti frullati e insaporire con burro e parmigiano reggiano. Mescolare **RAPIDAMENTE** il tutto a fuoco alto per 3 minuti e servire **SUBITO.**

(The following is an authentic Italian recipe from Alessia's kitchen. Read the recipe and answer the questions that follow.

Porcini mushroom tortelloni with black truffle

250 grams porcini mushroom tortelloni
1 small black truffle (about the size of a walnut)
2 tablespoons heavy cream
15 grams butter
1 cup parsley
1/2 glass of milk
50 grams parmesan (reggiano)
1. Chop the parsley coarsely. Add half a truffle, cutting it entirely into very thin slices. 2. Mix the other truffle, adding milk and subsequently

the heavy cream. 3. Cook the tortelloni exactly "al dente" in salty water. Drain well. 4. Add to the tortelloni, the parsley, the sliced truffle, and the previously mixed ingredients and flavor with butter and parmesan. Stir quickly on the stove on high for 3 minutes and serve immediately.)

Domande:[†]

1. Come dovrebbe essere tritato il prezzemolo?
2. La panna dovrebbe essere aggiunta prima o dopo del latte?
3. In che modo dovrebbe essere mescolato il tutto?
4. Quando dovrebbe essere servito il piatto?

Follow-up: Parlare della ricetta preferita con il compagno.

Questions:

1. How should the parsley be chopped?
2. Should the heavy cream be added before or after the milk?
3. How should the tortelloni be cooked?
4. When should the dish be served?

Follow-up: Share a favorite recipe with a classmate.

C. TEXTUAL ENHANCEMENT—SAMPLE MATERIALS FOR ROMANIAN

Target Structure: Gerundive

The following is a Romanian story, "Tinereţe fără de bătrâneţe şi viaţă fără de moarte" ("Eternal youth and eternal life"), retold by the instructor. Read the story and answer the questions that follow.

Au fost odată un împărat şi o împărăteasă. **Neputând** avea copii, s-au dus intro-zi să ceară sfat unui bătrân priceput dintr-un sat. Bătrânul, **văzând** marea lor dorinţă, le-a dat nişte leacuri, **zicându**-le:
—Numai un copil veţi avea. El va fi frumos dar nu veţi avea parte de el.
Auzind aceasta, împăratul s-a intristat, **gândindu**-se că fiul lui nu va fi lângă el cand va îmbătrâni. S-a bucurat până la urmă, **imaginându**-şi momentele frumoase care vor urma.
Zilele **trecând**, fiul împăratului s-a făcut mare. Era cel mai frumos şi mai inteligent copil din toată ţara, **citind** cărţi din leagăn, **crescând** intr-un an cât alţii in zece. **Făcându**-se mare, a vrut să plece de lângă părinţii lui, **venindu**-i dor de ducă.

(Once upon a time, there was and emperor and an empress. They couldn't have children, therefore they went one day to get advice from a wise old man in a village. The old man, seeing their great wish for a child, gave them some remedies, saying:
—You will have only one child. He will be handsome but you won't be able to rejoice at his presence.

[†] Instructor's Note: The questions were designed to encourage learners to pay attention to adverbs in the recipe.

Hearing this, the emperor grieved, thinking that he wouldn't have his son by his side when he would get old. He rejoiced in the end, thinking about the great moments he would live until then. As days passed by, the emperor's son grew up. He was the most handsome and the most intelligent child in the whole country, reading books when he was still a baby in the cradle, growing up in one year like others would in ten. When he was old enough, he wanted to leave his parents' home, feeling like going away.)

I. Intrebări

1. Cine nu putea avea copii?
2. Cine i-a ajutat pe împărat şi pe împărăteasă?
3. Ce a născut împărăteasa, o fată sau un băiat?
(Comprehension questions continue)

II. Follow up:

1. V-ar plăcea să fiţi fiul împăratului din povestea noastră?
2. Ce poveste v-a plăcut mai mult când eraţi copii?

I. Questions

1. Who couldn't have children?
2. Who helped the emperor and the empress?
3. The empress gave birth to a boy or a girl?

II. Follow-up

1. Would you like to be the emperor's son in our story?
2. What was your favorite story when you were a child?

D. TEXTUAL ENHANCEMENT—SAMPLE MATERIALS FOR FRENCH

Target Structure: Prepositions with Geographical Locations

This next text is taken from Wong's (2002) study. The target structures here are the French prepositions *à* or *en* with geographical locations. In French, the preposition *à* must be used with cities to say that one is *in* a specific city—*Marie est à Paris* (Mary is in Paris)—while *en* must be used with countries—*Marie est en France* (Mary is in France).

Note: This content may also be adapted for use in Italian and Spanish.

Please read this text carefully. You will be asked to complete a comprehension activity after you read the text.

La famille Pinard

Monsieur et Madame Pinard sont mariés depuis 40 ans. Ils habitent <u>à Marseille</u>, une belle ville <u>**en** France</u>. Monsieur et Madame Pinard ont trois enfants: Thomas, Lise et Patrick. Les Pinard sont très fiers de leurs enfants mais ils ne les voient pas souvent parce qu'ils travaillent dans des pays différents. Èvidemment, Monsieur et Madame Pinard s'ennuient beaucoup sans leurs enfants.

Thomas est le premier enfant de Monsieur et Madame Pinard. Il a 34 ans et il est marié. Présentement, Thomas est médecin <u>**en** Belgique</u>. Sa femme, Caroline, est Belge et elle est secrétaire pour un avocat. Thomas a rencontré sa femme dans un restaurant <u>**à** Bruxelles</u>. Ils n'ont pas d'enfants mais ils ont un chien qui s'appelle Fido.

Lise est célibataire et elle est le deuxième enfant des Pinard. Elle a 30 ans et elle est professeur de français <u>**en** Angleterre</u>. Lise aime beaucoup les langues et voyager. Lise parle français, italien, allemand et anglais. Actuellement, Lise habite <u>**à** Londres</u>, mais l'an prochain, elle va aller <u>**en** Chine</u> dans le cadre d'un programme d'échange. Elle va enseigner le français dans une université <u>**à** Shanghai</u> et en même temps, elle apprendra le chinois.

(Story continues)

(Mr. and Mrs. Pinard have been married for 40 years. They live in Marseille, a small city in France. Mr. and Mrs. Pinard have three children: Thomas, Lise and Patrick. The Pinards are very proud of their children but they do not see them often because they work in different countries. Evidently, Mr. and Mrs. Pinard miss their children.

Thomas is the first child of Mr. and Mrs. Pinard. He is 34 years old and he is married. Presently, Thomas is a doctor in Belgium. His wife, Caroline, is Belgian and she is a secretary for a lawyer. Thomas met his wife in a restaurant in Brussels. They don't have any children but they have a dog named Fido.

Lise is single and she is the second child of the Pinards. She is 30 years old and she is a French teacher in England. Lise likes languages and traveling very much. Lise speaks French, Italian, German and English. Currently, Lise lives in London but next year she will work in China in the context of an exchange program. She will teach French in a university in Shanghai and at the same time, she will learn Chinese.)

Activity A. Please circle the correct answer for each question based on the information you read about the Pinard family.

1. Where do Monsieur and Madame Pinard live?
   a. Nice   b. Paris   c. Marseille   d. Shanghai
2. Where does their son, Thomas the doctor, live?
   a. Greece   b. Belgium   c. France   d. Italy
3. Where did Thomas meet his wife, Caroline?
   a. Athens   b. Paris   c. Seville   d. Brussels
4. What is the profession of their daughter, Lise?
   a. secretary   b. lawyer   c. professor   d. psychologist

(Comprehension questions continue)

Activity B.[†] Guess whether the statements about your professor are true (*vrai*) or false (*faux*).

1. Votre professeur est allé(e) <u>**à** Paris</u>.   V   F
2. Votre professeur est déjà allé(e) <u>**en** Belgique</u>.   V   F
3. Votre professeur a étudié <u>**en** Italie</u>.   V   F
4. Votre professeur aimerait aller <u>**à** Londres</u>.   V   F
5. Votre professeur va aller <u>**en** Espagne</u> bientôt.   V   F

(1. Your professor went to Paris.   T   F
2. Your professor has already been to Belgium.   T   F
3. Your professor studied in Italy.   T   F
4. Your professor would like to go to London.   T   F
5. Your professor will go to Spain soon.   T   F)

[†] Instructor's Note: Have students complete the activity giving their best guesses. When they are done, give them the correct answers so they can check how well they guessed.

Activity C.‡ Complete the following statements with a <u>city</u> or <u>country</u>.

1. On peut se promener à Central Park à _____.
2. On peut visiter le musée d'Orsay **en** _____.
3. On peut manger le meilleur pizza **à** _____.
4. On peut voir les ruines romaines **en** _____.
5. On pourrait peut-être rencontrer le prince William **en** _____.
6. On pourrait voir les anciens palais des empereurs chinois **en** _____.
7. On pourrait peut-être voir la maison d'enfance de Jean-Claude Van Dam **en** _____.
8. On pourrait voir un spectacle de Céline Dion **à** _____.

(1. One can take a walk in Central Park in _____.
2. One can visit the d'Orsay museum in _____.
3. One can eat the best pizza at _____.
4. One can see Roman ruins in _____.
5. One could perhaps meet Prince William in _____.
6. On could see the old Chinese emperors' palaces in _____.
7. One could perhaps see Jean-Claude Van Dam's childhood house in _____.
8. One could see Celine Dion's show in _____.)

E. TEXTUAL ENHANCEMENT—SAMPLE MATERIALS FOR ENGLISH

Target Structure: Plural Markers

The following text is taken from Simard (2001). The target structures here are the plural forms of nouns.

The Collection

In my family, everybody collects something. My sister, likes to collect pieces of clothing such as a <u>SCARF</u>. She has <u>SCARVES</u> of different colors in her collection. She also likes to collect pictures of animals. Sometimes you can see one <u>WOLF</u> or many <u>WOLVES</u> in the picture. She does not have only one <u>SHELF</u> filled with pictures but five <u>SHELVES</u>. My younger brother likes to collect <u>LEAVES</u>. He likes to pick out his favorite <u>LEAF</u> on the ground during fall. My cat is a collector too. It collects <u>LIVES</u>!!! When it loses one <u>LIFE</u> it has eight others. My father likes to collect <u>KNIVES</u>. He tries to find the nicest <u>KNIFE</u> whenever he goes shopping.

My mother, on the other hand, likes to collect food in the refrigerator! It seems we have tons of <u>TOMATOES</u> and <u>POTATOES</u> in the refrigerator. When she sees one nice <u>TOMATO</u> or one nice <u>POTATO</u> at the grocery store, she always buys it for her collection. But these are not the only things she likes to collect. She also likes to collect <u>MANGOES</u>. A <u>MANGO</u> is a fruit. Sometimes, I think she collects "<u>NOES</u>" because she often tells me "<u>NO</u>" when I ask for something.

(Text continues)

---

‡ Instructor's Note: This follow-up activity is a referential structured input activity (see Chapter 6). This activity pushes learners to make the connection that when they see the preposition *à* they need to provide a city. When they see *en* they need to provide a country.

Follow-up: Do you have a collection? What about members of your family? Do they have collections? What type of things do you like to collect? What types of things do your family members collect? What is the strangest collection you have ever heard of or seen?

105

*Structured Input—
Sample Materials
for German*

F. STRUCTURED INPUT—SAMPLE MATERIALS FOR GERMAN

Target Structure: Simple Past

The processing problem here is low communicative value. Learners of German have trouble recognizing the past form because the concept of pastness is usually encoded by adverbs of time such as *früher* (earlier) or *heute* (today). The following activities were structured so that learners must pay attention to the verb forms in order to get the temporal reference. Note: this content may also be adapted for use in other languages.

Referential Activity A. Listen to the following sentences about Arnold Schwarzenegger's life. Indicate whether the action happened sometime in the past or today.

1. *früher / heute* (earlier / today)
2. *früher / heute*
3. *früher / heute*
4. *früher* / heute
5. *früher / heute*
6. *früher / heute*
7. *früher / heute*
8. *früher / heute*

Instructor's Script:

1. *Arnold treibt viel Sport.*
2. *Arnold ging Lebensmittel einkaufen.*
3. *Arnold macht jeden Tag das Bett.*
4. *Arnold backte sehr gern Kuchen.*
5. *Arnold trug den Müll'raus.*
6. *Arnold poliert jeden Samstag seinen Mercedes.*
7. *Arnold kaufte Adidas Turnschuhe.*
8. *Arnold arbeitete als Bademeister.*

1. Arnold does a lot of sports.
2. Arnold went grocery shopping.
3. Arnold makes his bed everyday.
4. Arnold liked to bake.
5. Arnold took the garbage out.
6. Arnold waxes his Mercedes Saturday.
7. Arnold bought Adidas sneakers.
8. Arnold was a lifeguard.

Affective Activity B. Find out if your classmates have done the following activities sometime in their past. If the activity applies to a classmate, he/she has to sign it. The student who has gathered all signatures first wins.

Was machtest du früher?   *Unterschrift*

1. *Last du viel?*   _____
2. *Sahst du viel fern?*   _____
3. *Fuhrst du viel Fahrrad?*   _____
4. *Machtest du viel Sport?*   _____
5. *Spieltest du Schach?*   _____
6. *Mochtest du Abba?*   _____

What did you do before?   Signature

1. Did you read a lot?   _____
2. Did you watch a lot of TV?   _____
3. Did you ride your bike a lot?   _____
4. Did you do a lot of sports?   _____
5. Did you play chess?   _____
6. Did you like Abba?   _____

G. STRUCTURED INPUT—SAMPLE MATERIALS FOR FRENCH

Target Structure: Direct Object Pronouns in French

The processing problem for direct object pronouns in French is that this form is not salient. Direct object pronouns in French tend to be in medial position, the least salient position so learners may skip over it. The following activities were designed to force learners to pay attention to direct object pronouns in order to extract meaning from input sentences. In other words, learners *must* pay attention to direct object pronouns and process them correctly in order to interpret sentences. Note that direct object pronouns are placed in initial position when possible to increase their perceptual saliency.

Referential Activity A. A French student at your university is talking about his very large family back in France. Listen to the descriptions of the student's family and decide which family member he is referring to. Pay attention to the object pronouns.

1. a. *sa mère*   b. *ses sœurs*   c. *son grand-père*
2. a. *son frère*   b. *sa grand-mère*   c. *ses parents*
3. a. *son grand-père* b. *sa sœur*   c. *ses parents*
4. a. *son père*   b. *son chien*   c. *ses grand parents*
5. a. *sa sœur*   b. *son père*   c. *ses chats*
6. a. *sa sœur*   b. *son père*   c. *ses chats*
7. a. *son neveu*   b. *sa nièce*   c. *ses frères*

Follow-up: *Et vous? Est-ce que vous vous entendez bien avec votre famille?*   *Oui   Non*

1. a. his mother   b. his sisters   c. his grandfather
2. a. his brother   b. his grandmother   c. his parents
3. a. his grandfather   b. his sister   c. his parents
4. a. his father   b. his dog   c. his grandparents
5. a. his sister   b. his father   c. his cats
6. a. his sister   b. his father   c. his cats
7. a. his nephew   b. his niece   c. his brothers

Follow-up: And you? Do you get along with your family?   Yes   No

Instructor's Script for Referential Activity A.

1. *Je ne **la** comprends pas.*
2. *Je **le** haïs.*
3. *Je **les** déteste.*
4. *Je **les** rencontre le dimanche.*
5. *Je **la** cherche en voiture pour aller à l'église.*
6. *Je **les** laisse dormir dans mon lit.*
7. *Je **le** paie pour promener mon chien.*

1. I don't understand **her.**
2. I hate **him.**
3. I hate **them.**
4. I'm meeting **them** Sunday.
5. I'm picking **her** up to go to church.
6. I let **them** sleep in my bed.
7. I pay **him** to walk my dog.

Affective Activity B. Read the following sentences about the most popular singers who are in the top ten of MTV and then give your opinion.

1. *Eminem entre dans le top directement en troisième position avec la chanson de son nouveau film.*
   Eminem, je _____.
   a. *le déteste*
   b. *le recommande*
   c. *le félicite*
2. *Jennifer Lopez lance sa nouvelle vidéo et se trouve en huitième position.*
   Jennifer Lopez, je _____.
   a. *la déteste*
   b. *la recommande*
   c. *la félicite*
3. *Les CDs de U2 sont célèbres; ils sont numéro cinq cette semaine.*
   Les CDs de U2, je _____.
   a. *les déteste*
   b. *les recommande*
   c. *les félicite*
4. *La musique country de Faith Hill se trouve en sixième position.*
   La musique country de Faith Hill, je _____.
   a. *la déteste*
   b. *la recommande*
   c. *la félicite*

1. Eminem enters in the top in third place with the song from his new film.
   Eminem, I _____.
   a. hate **him**
   b. recommend **him**
   c. congratulate **him**
2. Jennifer Lopez releases her new video and it is in eighth place.
   Jennifer Lopez, I _____.
   a. hate **her**
   b. recommend **her**
   c. congratulate **her**

3. U2's Cds are famous; they are number five this week.
   U2's Cds, I _____.
   a. hate **them**
   b. recommend **them**
   c. congratulate **them**
4. Faith Hill's country music is in sixth place.
   Faith Hill's country music, I _____.
   a. hate **it**
   b. recommend **it**
   c. congratulate **it**

H. STRUCTURED INPUT—SAMPLE MATERIALS FOR ENGLISH

Target Structure: third-person singular -s verb forms

The processing problem with this target structure is low communicative value. Learners of English have a tendency to drop the *-s* when the verb is in the third person singular form because the *-s* is redundant. The meaning of third person singular is already expressed by the subject, in many cases, the personal pronouns *he, she* or *it*. The following activities were designed so that learners are forced to pay attention to verb forms (i.e., *-s* or the absence of *-s*), in order to get meaning.

Referential Activity A. Jason is a college freshman in Dayton, Ohio, USA. In his political science class, Jason expresses views that are typically very different from the views of his classmates. Read the sentences below and indicate with an "X" whether each view expressed belongs to Jason or to Jason's classmates, and then indicate whether Jason is more conservative or more liberal than his classmates.

Jason . . .	His classmates . . .	
___	___	despises taxes to support the welfare system.
___	___	want to legalize marijuana.
___	___	thinks abortion should be illegal.
___	___	feel that public high schools should provide birth control.
___	___	support women's rights.
___	___	believes that same sex couples should not have children.

Choose One:

Jason is more liberal than his classmates. _____
Jason is more conservative than his classmates. _____

Affective Activity B. Read the following sentences. Are they true for a typical student at your school?

The typical student . . .	True	False
1. gets up at 7:00 a.m.	____	____
2. skips breakfast.	____	____
3. makes his bed everyday.	____	____
4. skips at least one class a week.	____	____
5. works part time.	____	____
6. cooks dinner every evening.	____	____

Your instructor will now read each statement and then ask you to raise your hand if you marked it as true. Someone should keep track of the responses on the board.

I. STRUCTURED INPUT—SAMPLE MATERIALS FOR SPANISH

Target Structure: ser and estar

OPTIONAL Explicit Information for *ser* and *estar*

English **to be** has several equivalents in Spanish: among them are **ser** and **estar**. In general, we use **ser** to tell who or what the subject is, or what it is really like. For example: *La niña es mona.*

In the example above, the speaker believes the child to be cute. That is, cuteness is a defining trait. It is a characteristic that the speaker believes the child to normally possess. Thus, the speaker uses **ser** with the adjective to describe the child.

In contrast with **ser**, **estar** is used with adjectives to describe a condition or state that a subject is in. This condition or states is viewed by the speaker to not be one of the subjects defining traits. For example: *La niña está muy mona.*

In the above example, the speaker does not believe that the child is typically cute. The speaker may even believe the opposite! On this particular occasion, the speaker perceives that cuteness is out of the ordinary for this child and thus uses **estar** with the adjective in order to convey this.

Referential Activity A.[†] Indicate whether the speaker considers the underlined adjective to be an inherent or defining characteristic of the entity described.

1. *El ex-presidente Bush es <u>conservador</u>.*   Sí   No
2. *Esta clase de español está <u>interesante</u>.*   Sí   No
3. *Madonna está <u>provocativa</u>.*   Sí   No
4. *Albert Einstein es <u>inteligente</u>.*   Sí   No

1. The ex-president Bush is <u>conservative</u>.   Yes   No
2. This Spanish class is (seems) <u>interesting</u>.   Yes   No
3. Madonna is (looks) <u>provocative</u>.   Yes   No
4. Albert Einstein is <u>intelligent</u>.   Yes   No

Affective Activity B. Which of the following are true for you? Check any that apply to your situation and then compare with your classmate.

___ 1. *Mi clase de español es mejor este semestre en comparación con la del semestre pasado.*

___ 2. *La comida de la cafetería es mejor en comparación con el año pasado.*

___ 3. *Mi clase de español está mejor ahora porque la serie* Destinos *se pone más interesante.*

___ 4. *La comida de la cafetería está mejor cuando se sirve caliente.*

___ 1. My Spanish class is better this semester in comparison with last semester's.

___ 2. The cafeteria food is better in comparison with last year.

[†] This activity is from Cheng (1995)

___ 3. My Spanish class is better now because the series *Destinos* has made it more interesting.
___ 4. The cafeteria food is better when it's served hot.

J. GCR TASKS—SAMPLE MATERIALS FOR ITALIAN

Target Structure: **da** *and* **per** *in Italian*

Note: This content may also be adopted for use in French: *depuis* vs. *pendant*. Direction lines for subsequent GCR Tasks should be similar and will not be repeated again here.

Directions: In pairs, you are to study correct and incorrect sentences illustrating <u>the expression of the use of time expressions with *da* and *per*</u>. You have different sentences. You must read your sentences to your partner. Do not show your sentences to your partner! Only read the sentences as many times as necessary! Work together as a team and decide on the basis of the correct and incorrect sentences what the rules for using the time expressions are. Choose one student to report your results to the rest of the class. Please speak only in <u>Italian</u> during this activity.

Activity A.

Student 1

Correct:	*Chiara studia l'italiano da cinque anni.*
Incorrect:	*Chiara studia l'italiano per cinque anni.*
Correct:	*Tom ha abitato in Canada per tre anni.*
Incorrect:	*Tom abita in Canada per tre anni.*
Correct:	Chiara has been studying Italian for five years.
Incorrect:	Chiara studies Italian for five years.
Correct:	Tom lived in Canada for three years.
Incorrect:	Tom lives in Canada for three years.

Student 2

Correct:	*Jane abita in California da tre mesi.*
Incorrect:	*Jane ha abitato in California da tre mesi.*
Correct:	*Victoria ha lavorato al caffè per quattro settimane.*
Incorrect:	*Victoria lavora al caffè per quattro settimane.*
Correct:	Jane has been living in California for three months.
Incorrect:	Jane lived in California for three months.
Correct:	Victoria worked at the café for four weeks.
Incorrect:	Victoria works at the café for four weeks.

Activity B. Please state the rules that underlie the use of *da* and *per* in Italian.

Instructor's Answer Key: *Da* is used with the present tense to mean "for" a duration of time. *Per* is used with the past tense to mean "for" a duration of time.

Referential Activity C.[†] Roberto is a perpetual student. He has been in school for eight years. He has taken numerous classes and is still taking many today. Read the

---

[†] Instructor's Note: This is a follow-up referential structured input activity used here to expose learners to more exemplars of the target form and to help them pay attention to *da* and *per* in order to get meaning.

following phrases to determine whether Roberto had taken these classes some time
in the past or is currently still taking them. Complete each sentences with either
studia (studies) or *ha studiato* (studied / has been studying).

Roberto . . .

_____ *la biologia per due anni.*
_____ *il francese da sei settimane.*
_____ *il portoghese da un anno.*
_____ *la filosofia per dieci settimane.*
_____ *la chimica per un anno.*
_____ *la letteratura italiana da due anni.*

Quali corsi ha seguito Roberto nel passato? _____
Quali corsi segue ancora? _____

Roberto . . .

_____ Biology for two years.
_____ French for six weeks.
_____ Portuguese for one year.
_____ Philosophy for ten weeks.
_____ Chemistry for one year.
_____ Italian Literature for two years.

What classes has Robert taken in the past? _____
What classes is he still taking? _____

Affective Activity D.[‡] Finish the following statements in your own way to
indicate how long you have been doing or did the following activities. Then
compare with the class. Did you all have similar responses?

1. *Abito a Columbus da* _____.
2. *Studio a Ohio State da* _____.
3. *Al liceo, ho studiato le lingue per* _____.

1. I've been living in Columbus for _____.
2. I've been studying at Ohio State for _____.
3. In high school, I studied languages for _____.

K. GCR TASKS—SAMPLE MATERIALS FOR SPANISH*

Target Structure: Subjunctive with Expressions of Doubt and Certainty

Note: This content may also be modified for use with French and Italian.

Activity A.

Student 1

Correct:	*No creo que el perro sea muy inteligente.*
Incorrect:	*No creo que el perro es muy inteligente.*
Correct:	*Es cierto que el serpiente necesita amigos.*
Incorrect:	*Es improbable que el serpiente necesita amigos.*
Correct:	I don't believe the dog is very intelligent.
Incorrect:	I don't believe the dog is very intelligent.

[‡] Instructor's Note: This is an affective structured input activity used here to give learners' additional opportunities to notice the target structure in input.

* These materials are taken from Farley (2000).

| Correct: | It is certain that the snake needs friends. |
| Incorrect: | It is not probable that the snake needs friends. |

Student 2

Correct:	*Yo creo que el pez es un animal aburrido.*
Incorrect:	*Yo creo que el pez sea un animal aburrido.*
Correct:	*No es verdad que el serpiente coma comida caliente.*
Incorrect:	*No es verdad que el serpiente come comida caliente.*

Correct:	I believe that the fish is a boring animal.
Incorrect:	I believe that the fish is a boring animal.
Correct:	It is not true that the snake eats hot food.
Incorrect:	It is not true that the snake eats hot food.

Activity B. Please write down the rules that underlie the use of the subjunctive based on the sentences you just examined. When must the subjunctive be used? When is the subjunctive not used?

Instructor's Answer Key: The subjunctive is used when there is doubt involved—for example, *Es dudoso que, No es verdad que* (It's doubtful that, It's not true that) and so on. The subjunctive is not used when "certainty" is expressed—for example, *Es cierto que, Es verdad que, Yo credo que* (It's certain that, It's true that, I believe that).

Referential Activity C.[†] The phrases below come from a magazine article about Leonardo DiCaprio. Indicate whether the author believes each idea or doubts each idea. Place an X under the opinion that fits with each phrase.

Creo que . . .	*Dudo que . . .*	
_____	_____	*sea un buen actor.*
_____	_____	*gana mucho dinero.*
_____	_____	*tiene una casa muy grande.*
_____	_____	*tenga una novia.*
_____	_____	*está contento con su carrera.*

I believe that . . .	I doubt that . . .	
_____	_____	he is a good actor.
_____	_____	he makes a lot of money.
_____	_____	he has a big house.
_____	_____	he has a fiancée.
_____	_____	he is happy with his career.

Activity D.[‡] You have probably heard something about the luxurious life of Bill Gates. Below are some statements about his home and his home life. Finish each of the three sentences underlined below using the phrases in parenthesis. Make sure to change the verb form when necessary. Then, place a check next to the statements that you agree with.

[†] Instructor's Note: This is a follow-up referential structured input activity used here to expose learners to more exemplars of the target form and to help them pay attention to verb forms in order to get meaning (i.e., doubt or certainty).

[‡] Instructor's Note: This is a follow-up output activity used here to give learners opportunities to practice using the target structures.

Es probable que su casa . . .

_____ *(tener aire acondicionado).*

_____ *(estar en un barrio seguro).*

Dudo que su casa . . .

_____ *(tener lavaplatos).*

_____ *(ser semejante a la casa de mis padres).*

No creo que Bill Gates . . .

_____ *(tener animales domésticos en su casa).*

_____ *(comer mucho en casa).*

It's probable that his house . . .

_____ (to have air conditioning).

_____ (to be in a safe neighborhood).

I doubt that his house . . .

_____ (to have dishwasher).

_____ (to be like my parents' house).

I don't believe that Bill Gates . . .

_____ (to have pets in his house).

_____ (to eat much at home).

L. GCR TASKS—SAMPLE MATERIALS FOR GERMAN

Target Structure: **kennen** *vs.* **wissen**

Note: This content may also be adopted for *savoir* vs. *connaître* in French, *conoscere* vs. *sapere* in Italian and *conocer* vs. *saber* in Spanish.

Activity A.

Student 1

Correct:	*Weißt du Ralfs Telefonnummer?*
Incorrect:	*Kennst du Ralfs Telefonnummer?*
Correct:	*Ich weiß, wo er wohnt.*
Incorrect:	*Ich kenne, wo er wohnt.*
Correct:	Do you know Ralf's phone number?
Incorrect:	Do you know Ralf's phone number?
Correct:	I know where he lives.
Incorrect:	I know where he lives.

Student 2

Correct:	*Ich kenne Frau Müller sehr gut.*
Incorrect:	*Ich weiß Frau Müller sehr gut.*
Correct:	*Kennst du diese Oper?*
Incorrect:	*Weißt du diese Oper?*
Correct:	I know Mrs Muller very well.
Incorrect:	I know Mrs Muller very well.
Correct:	Do you know this opera?
Incorrect:	Do you know this opera?

Activity B. Complete the following sentences to describe the rules that underlie the use of *kennen* vs. *wissen* in German

Rule 1: When you know a person, you use _____.
Rule 2: When you know how to do something, you use _____.
Rule 3: When you are familiar with someone/something, you use

_____.

Rule 4: When you know something as a fact, you use _____.
Rule 5: When you are acquainted with someone, you use _____.
Rule 6: When there is a direct object after the verb, this verb must be
_____, because it cannot be followed by a clause.

> Instructor's Answer Key: Rule 1: *kennen;* Rule 2: *wissen;* Rule 3: *kennen;* Rule 4: *wissen;* Rule 5: *kennen;* Rule 6: *kennen*

Activity C.[†]

Step 1. How well do you know your professor? Guess whether the statements about your professor are true (*Richtig*) or false (*Falsch*).

Herr/Frau _____ . . .

kennt den Präsidenten.	R	F
weiss, wer der Präsident ist.	R	F
weiß, wie man Sauerkraut kocht.	R	F
kennt Freiburg sehr gut.	R	F
weiß wo die Universität ist.	R	F
weiß, wann man wissen oder kennen benutzt.	R	F
kennt ihre Zensuren.	R	F
weiß, was Sie am Abend gemacht haben.	R	F
weiß, was Sie letzten Sommer gemacht haben.	R	F

Step 2. Now compare your guesses with a classmate. Were your answers similar or different?

Mr/Mrs. _____ . . .

knows the president.	T	F
knows who the president is.	T	F
knows how to cook sauerkraut.	T	F
knows Freiburg very well.	T	F
knows where the university is.	T	F
knows when to use *kennen* or *wissen*.	T	F
knows your grades.	T	F
knows what you did last night.	T	F
knows what you did last summer.	T	F

Activity C.[‡]

Nennen Sie zwei Dinge, die Sie kennen:
Nennen Sie zwei Dinge, die Sie wissen:

[†] Instructor's Note: This is a follow-up input activity to help learners to continue to pay attention to the target forms. Instructor will give the correct responses to see how well the class knows him/her.
[‡] Instructor's Note: This is a follow-up activity to expose learners to more target forms. Students could interview each other and report responses to the class.

Name two things that you know (that you are familiar with): \
Name two things that you know (that you know for a fact):

M. GCR TASKS—SAMPLE MATERIALS FOR ROMANIAN

Target Structure: The double direct object

Activity A.

Student A.

Correct: *Ea l-a chemat pe Marcel.* \
Correct: *Ea l-a chemat.* \
Incorrect: *Ea a chemat pe Marcel.*

Correct: She called him, Marcel. (double direct object, personal pronoun followed by preposition and noun) \
Correct: She called him. (single direct object, personal pronoun) \
Incorrect: She called Marcel. (single direct object, noun with preposition)

Student B.

Correct: *Mihaela și Simona le căutau pe Maria și Livia.* \
Correct: *Mihaela și Simona le căutau.* \
Incorrect: *Mihaela și Simona căutau pe Maria și Livia.*

Correct: Mihaela and Simona were looking for them, Maria and Livia. (double direct object, personal pronoun followed by preposition and nouns) \
Correct: Mihaela and Simona were looking for them. (single direct object, personal pronoun) \
Incorrect: Mihaela and Simona were looking for Maria and Livia. (single direct object, nouns with preposition)

Activity B. Complete the following sentences to describe the rules that underlie the use of the *pronouns and the nouns* when expressing animated direct objects:

Rule 1: When the animated direct object is expressed by a _____ preceded by a preposition, we have to double it by a personal pronoun. \
Rule 2: When the animated direct object is a _____, it is not compulsory to double it. \
Rule 3: It is incorrect to have in a phrase the animated direct object expressed only by a _____ preceded by a _____.

Instructor's Answer key: Rule 1: noun; Rule 2: pronoun; Rule 3: noun; preposition

---

Activity C.[†]

Step 1. How well do you know your teacher? Guess whether the statements about your teacher are true or false.

[†] Instructor's Note: This is a follow-up input activity. Instructor will give the correct responses to see how well the class knows him/her.

Profesoara noastră . . .

îi ajută pe studenţi. Ii ajută.	True	False
o pedepseşte pe Silvia, fata ei. O pedepseşte.	True	False
o sună rar pe mama ei. O sună rar.	True	False
îi iubeşte pe copii. Ii iubeşte.	True	False

Step 2. Now compare your guesses with a classmate. Were your answers similar or different?

Our teacher . . .
    helps students. She helps them.
    grounds Silvia, her daughter. She grounds her.
    rarely telephones her mom. She rarely telephones her.
    loves children. She loves them.

Activity D.

Part A. You are throwing a party and you think about inviting some of the people in your class. Name a few people you would invite.

EXAMPLE:
Eu o invit pe _____ (feminine singular).
Eu le invit pe _____ (feminine plural)
Eu îl invit pe _____ (masculine singular)
Eu îi invit pe _____ (masculine plural)

I (would) invite her.
I (would) invite them (feminine plural).
I would invite him.
I (would) invite them (masculine plural).

Part B. Now compare your phrases with a classmate. Were your answers similar or different? Who would you both invite to your party?

Noi o/îl/le/îi invităm pe _____.
We (would) invite _____.

Glossary

acquisition   refers to the processes that are involved in the creation of an implicit linguistic system.

acquisition orders   the sequential order in which learners master different grammatical forms. This order is said to be universal.

affective structured input activity   is a type of structured input activity that does not have a right or wrong answer. Learners are required to express an opinion, belief or some other affective response as they are engaged in processing information about the real world.

apperceived input   input that the learner has noticed in some way.

apperception   one of the stages of Gass's (1997) model of SLA. This is the stage where learners apperceive a particular feature of input or recognize that there is something out there to be learned.

attending to input   to pay attention to or notice the input in some way.

Audiolingual Method (ALM)   a teaching method widely used in the 1950s and 1960s based on behavioral psychology and structural linguistics. This method relied on memorization, repetition and drilling.

Cognitive-Code Method   a method of L2 instruction that advocates the learning of language rules through analysis. This method was developed as a reaction against ALM.

Communicative Language Teaching (CLT)   an approach to language instruction that views language as being intricately tied to the act of communication. The goal of CLT is to help L2 learners develop communicative competence.

communicative value   the degree to which a linguistic item contributes to understanding the overall referential meaning of an utterance or sentence. Items that are important for understanding the referential meaning of a message are high in communicative value. Conversely, items of low communicative value play less important roles in interpreting the meaning of messages.

comprehensible input   input that the learner can understand in some way.

Content-Based Instruction   uses the L2 as the medium of instruction rather than the object of instruction. In content-based classes, learners learn subject matters such as biology or history via the L2.

content words   words that carry significant meaning in an utterance, sometimes known as the "big words" (as opposed to function words like prepositions or articles).

corrective feedback   a pedagogical intervention that involves pointing out to a learner in some way that an error was made.

critical period hypothesis   the idea that a new language is more difficult to acquire completely after a certain point in one's development, usually thought to be around puberty.

dictogloss   a pedagogical activity that involves an instructor reading a passage to L2 learners that contain target structures. Learners are to take notes and then get into pairs or groups to try to reconstruct the passage.

Direct Method   a method of L2 instruction partly based on principles of L1 child acquisition. Rather than relying on the L1, learners are encouraged to make direct associations between new language forms and the meanings they encode.

elaboration (in relation to input enhancement)   refers to the depth and amount of time that is involved in implementing the enhancement technique.

explicit information   information about how a language works. Often, but not always, explicit information is provided via rules about how particular grammatical forms work.

explicit knowledge   conscious knowledge of rules that govern the use of grammatical structures.

explicitness (in relation to input enhancement)   refers to the sophistication and detail of attention-drawing device, e.g., explicit rule explanation.

focus-on-form   a term coined by Long (1991) to refer to pedagogical techniques that draw learners' attention to form within a meaningful context. Long introduced this term to distinguish these techniques from techniques that draw learners' attention to isolated language forms either separately from meaning or with no apparent regard for meaning. This second type is referred to as **focus-on-forms** (see next entry).

focus-on-forms   a term coined by Long (1991) to refer to instructional techniques that draw learners' attention to isolated linguistic forms either separately from meaning or with no regard to meaning (see also **focus-on-form**).

form   the surface features of language such as verbal and nominal morphology and functional items such as prepositions, articles, pronouns. Form can also refer to word form, i.e., *cat* is the word form for "a small feline."

form-meaning connection   the relationship between referential meaning and the way it is encoded linguistically, e.g., that *-s* means plural.

functional syllabus   a type of syllabus that is organized around different linguistic functions that L2 learners are expected to perform (e.g., giving compliments).

Garden Path technique   an instructional technique where learners are actually induced to make errors so that those errors could be pointed out to them in a systematic fashion.

grammar consciousness-raising task   an instructional technique that involves presenting L2 learners with L2 data for the purpose of solving a grammar puzzle. The goal of such a technique is to help learners arrive at some kind of **explicit knowledge** about the target form.

Grammar-Translation Method   an L2 teaching method that is based on the analysis of grammar and the translation of sentences and texts from learners' L1 to L2 and vice versa.

implicit linguistic system the learners' linguistic system that exists outside of conscious awareness.

input refers to samples of language that learners are exposed to in a communicative context or setting. It is language that has some kind of communicative intent. Also known as **primary linguistic data.**

input enhancement a term coined by Sharwood Smith (1991) to refer to deliberate attempts to make specific features of L2 input more salient in order to draw learners' attention to these features.

input flood a pedagogical technique in which L2 learners are purposefully exposed to multiple exemplars of a target grammatical form but nothing else is done to draw their attention to the forms. The input may be aural or written. The assumption here is that the sheer frequency of the form will help learners notice it.

input processing the process by which learners derive intake (or make form-meaning connections) from input as they try to comprehend a message.

intake the subset of input that has been processed in some way by the learner. Intake is created when learners make *form-meaning connections* from input and is the result of *input processing*.

interactional input input that is created as a result of conversational exchanges involving two or more people.

interlanguage refer to the systematic knowledge that learners have of their L2 at any given point in time during their L2 development.

language for display purposes refers to language that is used for the purpose of illustrating how a particular grammatical form is used. This is different from language for communication or communicative purposes where the purpose is to exchange information or negotiate meaning.

learning refers to a conscious knowledge of the rules of grammar that is a product of instruction (Krashen, 1982).

meaning refers to referential or real-world meaning, e.g., the meaning of *cat* is "a small feline."

negative evidence information about what is not possible in an L2. Explicit information could be considered a form of negative evidence.

non-interactional input input that occurs in the context of non-reciprocal discourse, e.g., listening to the radio.

noticed input/noticing input input that learners pay attention to in some way.

output language that learners access from their implicit system. It is language that learners produce to express meaning.

output processing the manner in which learners string together words and formal features of language to create utterances; it involves two main processes, access and production-based strategies (VanPatten, 2003).

positive evidence linguistic evidence (i.e., input) that does not contain any information about what is not possible in an L2. This is sometimes also known as naturalistic input (Trahey & White, 1993).

primary linguistic data linguistic data that contains communicative uses of instances or exemplars of the L2 (Schwartz, 1993). It is the same as how this book defines **input.**

rate of acquisition refers to the speed in which learners acquire certain features of an L2.

recasts are a type of corrective feedback. In this technique, the instructor rephrases the learner's incorrect utterance correctly.

redundancy occurs when the same meaning is expressed by both a formal feature of language and a content word in the utterance.

referential structured input activity are structured input activities that require learners to pay attention to form in order to get meaning. Referential activities have right or wrong answers.

route of acquisition refers to the order in which learners acquire certain features of an L2.

semantic value (inherent) refers to forms that have some kind of inherent meaning, e.g., the *-ed* in the verb *watched* has inherent semantic value because it expresses the meaning of pastness.

skill the ability to perform some act.

structural syllabus a syllabus that is organized around a series of grammatical structures.

structured input input that has been manipulated to push learners away from incorrect or non-optimal processing strategies towards more optimal ones.

structured input activities activities that use structured input to push learners to make correct-form meaning connections. There are two types of activities: **referential** and **affective** activities.

stages of development refer to how a learner acquires a particular linguistic feature of an L2 over time.

system change the process that entails accommodation of intake data into the developing system and restructuring of that system.

task-based syllabus a syllabus that is organized around a series of tasks (as opposed to grammatical structures or linguistic functions) that learners are expected to perform, e.g., take an opinion poll.

textual enhancement is a technique that involves manipulating the typographical features of a written text so that the perceptual salience of certain grammatical forms of that text are increased. This may be achieved by changing the font style, enlarging the character size, underlining, bolding, etc.

transparent form-function (or **form-meaning**) **relationship** means that the form has a relatively distinct meaning or function that corresponds to it, e.g. *-s* means plural.

Cited References

Alanen, R. (1995). Input enhancement and rule presentation in second language acquisition. In R. Schmidt (Ed.), *Attention and awareness in foreign language acquisition* (pp. 259–302). Honolulu: University of Hawaii.

Ausubel, D. (1968). *Educational psychology: A cognitive view.* New York: Holt, Rinehart and Winston.

Barcroft, J. (2000). The effects of sentence writing as semantic elaboration on the allocation of processing resources and second language lexical acquisition. Unpublished Doctoral Dissertation, University of Illinois at Urbana-Champaign.

Bardovi-Harlig, K., & Reynolds, D. (1995). The role of lexical aspect in the acquisition of tense and aspect. *TESOL Quarterly, 29,* 107–131.

Benati, A. (2004). The effects of structured input activities and explicit information on the acquisition of Italian tense. In B. VanPatten (Ed.), *Processing instruction: Theory, research and commentary.* Mahwah, NJ: Erlbaum.

Birdsong, D. (1999). Whys and why nots of the critical period hypothesis for second language learning. In D. Birdsong (Ed.), *Second language acquisition and the critical period hypothesis* (pp. 1–22). Mahwah, NJ: Erlbaum.

Cadierno, T. (1995). Formal instruction in processing perspective: An investigation into the Spanish past tense. *The Modern Language Journal, 79,* 179–194.

Canale, M. (1983). From communicative competence to communicative language pedagogy. In J. Richards and R. Schmidt (eds.), *Language and communication.* London: Longman.

Canale, M., & Swain, M. (1980). Theoretical bases of communicative approaches to second language teaching and testing. *Applied Linguistics, 1,* 1–47.

Chastain, K. (1976). *Developing second language skills: Theory to practice (2nd edition).* Chicago: Rand McNally.

Cheng, A. (1995). Grammar instruction and input processing: The acquisition of Spanish *ser* and *estar.* Unpublished doctoral thesis, University of Illinois at Urbana-Champaign.

Corder, S. P. (1981). *Error analysis and interlanguage.* Oxford: Oxford University Press. (Reprinted from Corder, S. P. (1967). The significance of learners' errors. *International Review of Applied Linguistics, 5,* 161–170.)

Doughty, C. (2003). Instructed SLA: Constraints, compensation, and enhancement. In C. Doughty & M. Long, Eds.), *The Handbook of second language acquisition* (pp. 256–310). Oxford: Blackwell.

Doughty, C. & Williams, J. (1998). *Focus on form in classroom second language acquisition.* Cambridge: Cambridge University Press.

Doughty, C., & Williams, J. (1998). Pedagogical choices in focus on form. In C. Doughty & J. Williams (Eds.), *Focus on form in second language classroom acquisition* (pp. 197–261). Cambridge, MA: Cambridge University Press.

Ellis, R. (1986). *Understanding second language acquisition.* Oxford: Oxford University Press.

Ellis, R. (1989). Are classroom and naturalistic acquisition the same? A study of the classroom acquisition of German word order rules. *Studies in Second Language Acquisition, 11,* 305–328.

Ellis, R. (1990). Instructed second language acquisition. Oxford: Blackwell.

Ellis, R. (1992). Learning to communicate in the classroom: A study of two language learners' requests. *Studies in Second Language Acquisition, 14,* 1–23.

Ellis, R. (1993). The structural syllabus and second language acquisition. *TESOL Quarterly, 27,* 91–113.

Ellis, R. (1994). *The study of second language acquisition.* Oxford: Oxford University Press.

Ellis, R. (1997). *SLA research and language teaching.* Oxford: Oxford University Press.

Farley, D. (2000). *The relative effects of processing instruction and meaning-based output instruction on L2 acquisition of the Spanish subjunctive.* Unpublished doctoral thesis, University of Illinois at Urbana-Champaign.

Fotos, S. (1993). Consciousness raising and noticing through focus on form: Grammar task performance vs. formal instruction. *Applied Linguistics, 14,* 385–407.

Fotos, S. (1994). Integrating grammar instruction and communicative language use through grammar consciousness-raising tasks. *TESOL Quarterly, 28,* 323–351.

Fotos, S. (2002). Structure-based interactive tasks for the EFL grammar lesson. In E. Hinkel and S. Fotos (Eds.), *New perspectives on grammar teaching in second language classrooms* (pp. 135–154). Mahwah, New Jersey: Erlbaum.

Fotos, S., & Ellis, R. (1991). Communicating about grammar: A task-based approach. *TESOL Quarterly, 25,* 605–628.

Fotos, S., Homan, R., & Poel, C. (1994). *Grammar in mind: Communicative English for fluency and accuracy.* Tokyo: Logos.

Gaonac'h, D. (1987). *Théorie d'apprentissage et acquisition d'une langue étrangère.* Paris: Hatier.

Gass, S. (1997). *Input, interaction, and the second language learner.* Mahwah, NJ: Erlbaum.

Harley, B. (1993). Instructional Strategies and SLA in early French immersion. *Studies in Second Language Acquisition, 15,* 245–260.

Harley & Swain (1984). The interlanguage of immersion students and its implication for second language teaching. In A. Davies, C. Criper, & A. Howatt (Eds.), *Interlanguage* (pp. 291–311). Edinburgh: Edinburgh University Press.

Harley, B., & Wang, W. (1997). The critical period hypothesis: Where are we now? In A. M. B. de Groot & J. F. Kroll (Eds.), *Tutorials in bilingualism: Psycholinguistic perspectives* (pp. 19–51). Mahwah, NJ: Erlbaum.

Hinkel, E., & Fotos, S. (2002). *New perspectives on grammar teaching in second language classrooms.* Mahwah, NJ: Erlbaum.

Huot. D. (1995). Observer l'attention. In R. Schmidt (Ed.), *Explicit and implicit processes in foreign language acquisition* (pp. 85–126). Honolulu: University of Hawai'i at Manoa.

Jourdenais, R., Ota, M., Stauffer, S., Boyson, B., & Doughty, C. (1995). Does textual enhancement promote noticing? A think-aloud protocol analysis. In R. Schmidt (Ed.), Attention and awareness in second language learning (Technical Report 9) (pp. 183–216). Honolulu: University of Hawaii, Second Language Teaching and Curriculum Center.

Kaplan, M. A. (1987). Developmental patterns of past-tense acquisition among foreign language learners of French. In B. VanPatten, T. R. Dvorak, & J. F. Lee (Eds.), Foreign language learning: A research perspective (pp. 52–60). Cambridge, MA: Newbury House.

Kramsch, C. (2000). Second language acquisition, applied linguistics, and the teaching of foreign languages. *The Modern Language Journal, 84,* 311–326.

Krashen, S. (1981). *Second language acquisition and second language learning.* Oxford: Pergamon.

Krashen, S. (1982). *Principles and practice in second language acquisition.* New York: Pergamon.

Krashen (1983). Second language acquisition theory and the preparation of teachers. In J. Alatis, H. Stern and P. Strevens (Eds.), *Applied linguistics and the preparation of teachers: Toward a rationale.* Washington D.C.: Georgetown University Press.

Krashen (1985). *The input hypothesis: Issues and implications.* London: Longman.

Larsen-Freeman, D. (1986). *Techniques and principles in language teaching.* Oxford: Oxford University Press.

Larsen-Freeman, D., & Long, M. (1991). An *introduction to second language acquisition.* New York: Longman.

Lee, J. F., & VanPatten, B. (2003). *Making communicative language teaching happen (2nd edition).* New York: McGraw-Hill.

Leeser, M. J. (2003). *Second language comprehension and processing grammatical form: The effects of topic familiarity, mode, and pausing.* Unpublished doctoral dissertation, University of Illinois at Urbana-Champaign.

Lenneberg, E. (1964). *New directions in the study of language.* Cambridge, Mass: M.I.T. Press.

Leow, R. (1998). The effects of amount and type of exposure on adult learners' L2 development in SLA. *The Modern Language Journal, 82,* 49–68.

Leow, R. (2001). Do learners notice enhanced forms while interacting with the L2?: An online and offline study of the role of written input enhancement in L2 reading. *Hispania, 84,* 496–509.

Lightbown, P. (1983). Exploring relationships between developmental and instructional sequences in L2 acquisition. In H. Seliger & M. Long (Eds.), *Classroom-oriented research in second language acquisition* (pp. 217–243). Rowley, MA: Newbury House.

Lightbown, P. (1985). Great expectations: Second-language acquisition research and classroom teaching. *Applied Linguistics, 6,* 173–189.

Lightbown, P. (1991). What have we here? Some observations on the role of instruction in second language acquisition. In R. Phillipson, E. Kellerman, L. Selinker, M. Sharwood Smith, and M. Swain (Eds.), *Foreign/second language pedagogy research: A commemorative volume for Claus Faerch.* Clevedon: Multilingual Matters.

Lightbown, P. (1998). The importance of timing in focus on form. In C. Doughty and J. Williams (Eds.), *Focus on form in classroom second language acquisition.* Cambridge: Cambridge University Press.

Lightbown, P. (2000). Classroom SLA research and second language teaching. *Applied Linguistics, 21,* 431–462.

Lightbown & Spada (1990). Focus-on-form and corrective feedback in communicative language teaching. *Studies in Second Language Acquisition, 12,* 429–447.

Lightbown, P. M. & Spada, N. (1999). *How languages are learned.* Revised edition. Oxford: Oxford University Press.

Long, M. (1983). Does second language instruction make a difference? A review of research. *TESOL Quarterly, 17,* 359–382.

Long, M. H. (1988). Instructed interlanguage development. In L. Beebe (Ed.), *Issues in second language acquisition: Multiple perspectives* (pp. 115–141). Rowley, MA: Newbury House.

Long, M. (1990). The least a theory of second language acquisition has to explain. *TESOL Quarterly, 24,* 649–66.

Long, M. (1991). Focus on form: A design feature in language teaching methodology. In K. de bot, R. Ginsberg, & C. Kramsch (Eds.), *Foreign language research in cross-cultural perspectives* (pp. 39–52). Amsterdam: John Benjamins.

Long, M., & Porter, P. (1985). Group work, interlanguage talk and second language acquisition. *TESOL Quarterly, 19,* 207–228.

Loprete, C. (2001). *Iberoamérica: Historia de su civilizaci'on y cultura. 4th ed.* Upper Saddle River, NJ: Prentice Hall.

Loschky, L., & Bley-Vroman, R. (1990). Creating structure-based communication tasks for second language development. *University of Hawaii Working Papers in ESL, 9,* 161–212.

Lyster, R. (1998). Recasts, repetition and ambiguity in L2 classroom discourse. *Studies in Second Language Acquisition, 20,* 51–81.

Musumeci, D. (1997). *Breaking tradition.* New York: McGraw-Hill.

Nunan, D. (1993). *Introducing discourse analysis.* London: Penguin.

Omaggio-Hadley, A. (2001). *Teaching language in context.* Boston: Heinle & Heinle.

Overstreet, M. (1998). Text enhancement and content familiarity: The focus of learner attention. *Spanish Applied Linguistics, 2,* 229–258.

Overstreet, M. (2000). *The effects of textual enhancement over time on intake and production.* Paper delivered at the annual meeting of the American Association for Applied Linguistics. Vancouver, March 2000.

Pica, T. (1987). Interlanguage adjustments as an outcome of NS-NNS negotiated interaction, *Language Learning, 34,* 91–109.

Richards, J. C. , & Rodgers, T. S. (2001). *Approaches and methods in language teaching 2nd edition.* Cambridge: Cambridge University Press.

Ridenour, F. (1967). *So what's the difference?* Ventura, CA: Regal Books.

Rivers, W. (1987). *Interactive language teaching.* Cambridge: Cambridge University Press.

Rosa, E. & O'Neill, M. (1999). Explicitness, intake and the issue of awareness: Another piece to the puzzle. *Studies in Second Language Acquisition, 21,* 511–556.

Rutherford, W., & Sharwood Smith, M. (1985). Consciousness-raising and universal grammar. *Applied Linguistics, 6,* 274–282.

Saint-Exupéry, A. (1943). *Le Petit prince.* New York: Harcourt Inc.

Sanz, C. and Morgan-Short, K. (2002). *Must computers deliver explicit feedback?* An Empirical Study. Paper delivered at the conference on Form-meaning Connections in Second Language Acquisition. Chicago, February 21–24, 2002.

Savignon. S. (1998). *Communicative competence: Theory and classroom practice (2nd edition).* New York: McGraw-Hill.

Schmidt, R. W. (1990). The role of consciousness in second language learning. *Applied Linguistics, 11,* 129–158.

Schmidt, R. W. (1993). Awareness and second language acquisition. *Annual Review of Applied Linguistics, 13,* 206–26.

Schmidt, R. W. (1995). Consciousness and foreign language learning: A tutorial on the role of attention and awareness in learning. In R. Schmidt (Ed.), *Attention and awareness in foreign language learning* (pp. 1–64). University of Hawaii at Manoa: Second Language Teaching and Curriculum Center.

Schmidt, R. (2001). Attention. In P. Robinson (ed.), *Cognition and second language instruction* (pp. 3–32). Cambridge: Cambridge University Press.

Schwartz, B. D. (1993). On explicit and negative data affecting competence and linguistic behavior. *Studies in Second Language Acquisition, 15,* 147–163.

Selinker, L. (1972). Interlanguage. *International Review of Applied Linguistics, 10,* 209–31.

Sharwood Smith, M. (1981). Consciousness-raising and the second language learner. *Applied Linguistics, 2,* 159–168.

Sharwood Smith, M. (1991). Speaking to many minds: On the relevance of different types of language information for the L2 learner. *Second Language Research, 7,* 118–132.

Shook, J. D. (1994). FL/L2 reading, grammatical information, and the input to intake phenomenon. *Applied Language Learning, 5,* 57–93.

Simard, D. (2001). Effet de la mise en évidence textuelle sur l'acquisition de différente marques du pluriel en anglais langue seconde auprès de jeunes francophones de première secondaire. Doctoral dissertation, Université Laval, Québec.

Simard, D., & Wong, W. (2004). Language awareness and its multiple possibilities for the L2 classroom. *Foreign Language Annals, 37,* 96–110.

Simonds, N., & Swartz, L. (2002). *Moonbeams, dumplings and dragon boats.* New York: Harcourt, Inc.

Spada, N. (1997). The relationship between instructional differences and learning outcomes: A process-product study of communicative language teaching. *Applied Linguistics, 8,* 137–155.

Swain, M. (1985). Communicative competence: some roles of comprehensible input and comprehensible output in its development. In S. M. Gass & C. Madden (Eds.), *Input in second language acquisition* (pp. 235–253). Rowley, MA: Newbury House.

Swain, M. (1995). Three functions of output in second language learning. In G. Cook & B. Seidlhofer (Eds.), *Principle and practice in applied linguistics* (pp. 125–144). Oxford: Oxford University Press.

Swain, M. (1998). Focus on form through conscious reflection. C. Doughty and J. Williams (Eds.), *Focus on form in classroom second language acquisition* (pp. 64–81). Cambridge: Cambridge University Press.

Thompson, G. (1996). Some misconceptions about communicative language teaching. *ELT Journal, 50,* 9–15.

Tomasello, M., & Herron, C. (1989). Feedback for language transfer errors: The garden path technique. *Studies in Second Language Acquisition, 11,* 384–395.

Tomlin, R. S. & Villa, V. (1994). Attention in cognitive science and second language acquisition. *Studies in Second Language Acquisition, 16,* 183–203.

Trahey, M. & White, L. (1993). Positive evidence and preemption in the second language classroom. *Studies in Second Language Acquisition, 15,* 181–204.

Ur, P. (1988). *Grammar practice activities: A practical guide for teachers.* Cambridge: Cambridge University Press.

VanPatten, B. (1996). *Input processing and grammar instruction.* Norwood, NJ: Ablex.

VanPatten, B. (1999). What is second language acquisition and what is it doing in my department? *ADFL Bulletin, 30,* 49–53.

VanPatten, B. (2002). Communicative classrooms, processing instruction, and pedagogical norms. In S. Gass et. al. (Eds.), *Pedagogical norms for second and foreign language learning and teaching: Studies in honor of Albert Valdman* (pp. 105–118). Amsterdam: John Benjamins.

VanPatten, B. (2003). *From input to output: A teacher's guide to second language acquisition.* New York: McGraw-Hill.

VanPatten, B. (2004). *Fundamental similarity and contextual difference in child first language acquisition and adult second language acquisition.* M.S. 2004.

VanPatten, B. & T. Cadierno. (1993). Input processing and second language acquisition: A role for instruction. *Modern Language Journal, 77,* 45–57.

VanPatten, B., & Mandall, P. (1999). How type of structure influences the ways in which L2 learners render grammaticality judgments. Paper presented at the annual meeting of the AAAL, Stamford, Connecticut, 1999.

VanPatten, B. & Oikennon, S. (1996). Explanation versus structured input in processing instruction. *Studies in Second Language Acquisition, 18,* 495–510.

VanPatten, B., & Wong, W. (2004). Processing instruction and the French causative: a replication. In B. VanPatten (Ed.), *Processing Instruction: Theory, research and commentary.* Mahwah, NJ: Erlbaum.

Williams, J., & Evans, J. (1998). What kind of focus and on which forms? In C. Doughty & J. Williams (Eds.), *Focus on form in second language classroom acquisition* (pp. 139–155). Cambridge, MA: Cambridge University Press.

Wing, B. H. (1987). The linguistic and communicative functions of foreign language teacher talk. In B. VanPatten, T. R. Dvorak, & J. F. Lee (Eds.), *Foreign language learning: A research perspective* (pp. 158–173). Cambridge, MA: Newbury House.

Wong, W. (2001). Modality and attention to meaning and form in the input. *Studies in Second Language Acquisition, 23,* 345–368.

Wong, W. (2002a). Linking form and meaning: Processing Instruction. *The French Review, 76,* 236–264.

Wong, W. (2002b). *Decreasing attentional demands in input processing: A textual enhancement study.* Paper presented at the annual meeting of the Second Language Research Forum (SLRF), Toronto, Canada. October 3–6, 2002.

Wong, W. (2004a). The nature of processing instruction. In B. VanPatten (Ed.), *Processing Instruction: Theory, research and commentary.* Mahwah, NJ: Erlbaum.

Wong, W. (2004b). Processing instruction in French: The roles of explicit information and structured input. In B. VanPatten (Ed.), *Processing instruction: Theory, research and commentary.* Mahwah, NJ: Erlbaum.

Wong, W., & Simard, D. (2001). La saisie: Cette grande oubliée! *La Revue AILE (Acquisition et Interaction en Langues Étrangères), 14,* 59–86.

Wong, W., & VanPatten, B. (2003). The evidence is IN: Drills are OUT. *Foreign Language Annals, 36,* 403–423.

Index

NOTE: Page numbers with an n, f, or t indicate a note, illustration, or table.